Dear Fred

Merry Christmas
2015

Michael Marie
+
Jessica

1

Writeman Enterprises
Tallahassee, Florida
www.writeman.com

First printing 2015

Printed in the United States of America

ISBN: 978-154679494

Cover Design by Bonnie Mutchler

Baseball was, is, and always will be, to me,
the best game in the world. "
*   -Babe Ruth-*

This book is dedicated to the memory of H. W. Crosby.

Thanks Pop for teaching Bob and me to love baseball.

In the Big Inning God Created Baseball

Table of Contents

In the Big Inning: God Created Baseball

Introduction

How do we know God loves baseball? It's a simple deduction. In the Big Inning God created baseball. Of course the Bible puts it this way: "In the beginning God created heaven and earth." But, the "beginning" was the "biggest inning" for the universe. If you read down a few verses in the creation story you see how God laid the groundwork for baseball. It says "God said "…let dry ground appear. And it was so. God called the dry ground "land."

Don't get the connection? Let me clarify it for you. It is my understanding that you can't go anywhere on land without being in the middle of a baseball field. Your house is built on a baseball field. The school you attended is constructed over a baseball diamond. Your church, your office building, swimming pool, everything is built over a baseball diamond. Even football fields are created over baseball diamonds.

Confused? Here's the answer to the mystery. You see, when you stand at home plate on any baseball field or stadium you see two lines extending outward from home plate. One of them is the first base line that extends all the way to the right field fence. The other is the third base line that extends to the left field fence. The fence runs from the right field line to the left field line completing the ballpark.

Here's the little known fact. These foul lines never end. The outfield fence or stands are there to keep the outfielders from having to chase the ball after a batter hits it over the fence for a home run. But, the foul lines don't end at the fence they continue on out of the park across the road, through the city, state, across the rivers, oceans and on to other countries. Of course they aren't drawn on the ground. They are invisible once they pass the fence. So, someone standing in his or her front yard in Chicago may be standing between the foul lines of a ball park that faces northwest and is located in Tallahassee, FL. And the invisible foul lines have extended all the way to Illinois.

Likewise someone in Oregon may be standing in fair territory of a park in Chicago that faces west. So, no matter where you go you are in a ballpark as you crisscross this network of invisible foul lines. That's probably where the phrase "give me a ballpark figure" comes from. But, I envision the foul lines of all these different ballparks in every city and state in America crisscrossing, overlapping and duplicating ballparks ad infinitum. You may not see those invisible lines that started at home plate, but they would be extensions of a ballpark somewhere. And many of those would-be-ballparks may have houses or businesses built over them. Okay so maybe we've indulged in a little levity. But, it has you thinking about how baseball and baseball terms really permeate our environment.

It's obvious that God loved baseball enough to create it in the big inning. The land He made is now full of baseball fields. It's also why there are so many life lessons we can learn from the game of baseball to use in our daily lives when we apply Bible scriptures to them.

So hang on because here come 100 life lessons from Baseball and the Bible!

Diamond Lesson #1

The Big Inning

In the beginning God created the heavens and the earth.   Genesis 1:1

Everything has to start somewhere and at sometime. Close your eyes and try to blank out everything, all the distractions, every activity that is going on around you. Try to picture nothingness. Darkness. Loneliness. Allow nothing from today's world to creep in. Hard to do? Right, because our minds are active and filled with all sorts of actions and activities.

That's how it was in the beginning. God created the heavens and the earth out of a whole bunch of nothing. And that's where baseball potentially got its start. When God said "let dry ground appear" and "He called the dry ground 'land' the stage was set. Now baseball fields could be built. That was the big inning for the game of baseball. A diamond in the rough, so to speak, was born.

Winning the first inning of a baseball game is important. To get off to a good start and score more runs than the other team in the beginning gives your team a positive start and boosts the chances for victory. But as Yogi Berra would say, "It ain't over 'til it is over." The game is not already won.

Each day God provides us with a fresh 24-hours. Each day is a whole new ball game unlike any other one before. If we start off with prayer and Bible reading we win the first inning. The day is not over. Things may happen that can defeat us. We may have to rally to win the day. Winning the first inning will provide lessons that fortify a comeback effort when needed. Put your heavy hitters at the plate in the beginning: Start

your lineup with Prayer; Bible Reading; and Planning your day.

Big Inning Quote #1:

Baseball is a beautiful game from the first inning on:

"I like to look down on a field of green and white, a summertime land of Oz,

a place to dream. I've never been unhappy in a ball park."

-Jim Murray-
Los Angeles Times

Diamond Lesson #2

Starting Pitcher

Everything got started in Him and finds its purpose in Him.
Colossians 1:17 (The Message)

In a baseball game the starting pitcher is in control. Nothing happens until he throws the ball. Until the pitcher throws it, the game can't start. The hitter can't hit the ball or miss it or take the pitch until it is thrown. On the mound the pitcher peers in for a sign from the catcher, but if he doesn't feel comfortable with the pitch he can change it.

Yet, the pitcher is only in control until he throws it. Then, he is at the mercy of the batter's decision and possibly the fielding expertise of his teammates. Even in this age of specialists with long relief guys, middle relievers, set up men and closers, being the starting pitcher is still prestigious.

John Smoltz started 361 games in his first 13 years with the Atlanta Braves. From 2002-04 he was the closer in 310 games. In 2005, his 18th season, Smoltz asked to return to being a starting pitcher. It would be a dramatic change. Not many pitchers go from closer to starter. Hardly any go from starter to closer and back to starter. Along the way he realized no matter what pitching role he was performing he was not in control and that knowledge led Smoltz to put his faith in Jesus Christ.

John Smoltz said: "Some people think, I'll wait until all the problems are behind me and then I'll turn my life around. But someone told me, 'You may never see that day.' Thinking that through, Smoltz decided to put his faith in Christ and, secure in that decision, he enjoyed a long, successful, Hall of Fame career.

Jesus is the starting pitcher who needs no relief. He can be counted on to go the distance. He's there from the start of the season to the final game. *Colossians 1:17 (NLT)* says: *He existed before everything else began, and He holds all creation together.* He is in control no matter whether we acknowledge it or not.

As the apostle Paul says in *Colossians 1:15 Christ is the visible image of the Invisible God.* Christ is first in everything. To continue the starting pitcher analogy: He is the opening day starter---the first day of our lives--- and he's the seventh game of the World Series starter---the final day for each of us.

A lifetime is a long season. We will make mistakes along the way, but choosing Jesus as our starting pitcher ensures victory. Paul said: *He made peace with everything in heaven and on earth by means of His blood on the cross.* The errors we make are compensated for by His blood shed for us on the cross.

.

Big Inning Baseball Quote #2:

Starting pitchers closely observe starting pitchers

"Every pitch has a purpose. Sometimes he knows what he's going to throw two pitches ahead. He makes it look like the guys are swinging foam bats."

**-John Smoltz-
on Greg Maddux**

Diamond Lesson #3

The Lineup

God has given each of you some special abilities, be sure to use them to help each other passing on to others God's many kinds of blessings.   1 Peter 4:10

Decisions! Decisions! They start for the Major League manager or the College head coach before the game begins when he has to decide on a lineup. There are lots of factors that go into making out the lineup card he hands over to the umpires at home plate before the game.

Who will play and who will bat in each position are the two things it boils down to. He must consider if a lefty or a right-hander is pitching. Who's hitting well and who isn't. Does anybody really hit this starting pitcher exceptionally well? Whose glove is needed in this game? As well as a few other extraneous things to ponder.

Redsox Manager Terry Francona had an on-going lineup dilemma during the 2004 season. Who should bat third and who should follow at cleanup. Both Manny Ramirez and David Ortiz preferred hitting third for an obvious reason---protection. Whichever of these imposing figures was in the on-deck circle meant the one batting would get better pitches to hit and would not be pitched around. Francona said, "You can't let your players make out the batting order. But, if there is a comfort zone and they're really good players I want them to feel good about themselves." Francona was able to juggle the situation so that the lineup reflected what was best for the team. Good enough to become World Champions.

A player's value is determined by what he contributes to the team. Yet, we don't have to be superstars to break into God's lineup. The starting lineup of disciples who were closest to Jesus is described by John MacArthur in *Twelve Ordinary Men,* "They were mere fishermen and working-class nobodies." He adds: "They were the first preachers of the new covenant."

Since the "twelve" were not glib, sophisticated public speakers those who were called " the elite" disrespected them and put no credence in their sermons. Their message was simple and penetrating and won over multitudes of people because of the passion they brought to the platform. Each one of the twelve knew his role and performed it well.

Peter, the simple fisherman who started the church as we have come to know it, is a prime example of how God wants us to use our abilities to be team players and to serve others. We weren't given special talents solely for our own benefit. Jesus described the role that is laid out for us when he said, "Let your good deeds shine out for all to see, so that everyone will praise your heavenly Father." (Matthew 5:16).

Each of us is in God's lineup for a reason!

Big Inning Baseball Quote #3:

The lineup tells a lot about the game:

"It has been said that baseball exemplifies a tension in the American mind, the constant pull between our atomistic individualism and our yearning for Community…The very fact there is a lineup suggests the one-thing-at-a-time aspect of the game. But, baseball is really always a one-against-nine game."

---George F. Will---
Men at Work: The Craft of Baseball

Diamond Lesson #4

Who's on First?

A good name is better than precious ointment.   *Ecclesiastes 7:1*

Lou Costello: " Look, Abbott, if you're the manager you must know all the players."

Bud Abbott: "I certainly do."

Costello: "…So tell me their names."

Abbott: "Well on the bags we have, Who's on first, What's on second, and I Don't Know is on third."

Costello: "Are you the manager and you don't know these fellows names?"

Abbott: " Well, I should."

Costello: "Then, who's on first?"

Abbott: "Yes."

Costello: "I mean the fellow's name."

Abbott: "Who."

Costello: "The guy on first."

Abbott: "Who."

That Bud Abbott and Lou Costello routine has been around for over 70 years and it's still funny. Of course, it is all about names. There are certain baseball names that carry a strong reputation with them. When you hear the name Nolan Ryan, it just automatically starts the movie rolling in your mind of him blazing a fastball past hapless hitters. Babe Ruth triggers pictures of the big guy making contact, looking up to follow the ball's flight, then starting that practiced jog around the bases. The fans always knew

26

"Who" was pitching and "Who" was playing right field when those two were in a game. Their reputations were well known.

In *Ecclesiastes* King Solomon said that a good name is extremely important. He's talking about your reputation. It's not a matter of whether "Joe" is a better name than "John." It's all about the reputation we build that governs how people react when they hear our name.

Solomon had built quite a reputation. In addition to being the wisest king in the history of Israel, he was a botanist, zoologist, architect, poet, and philosopher (*NLT*, pg. 505). He was unparalleled in the ancient world. News of his extraordinary intelligence circulated among cities everywhere.

The Queen of Sheba heard all this and journeyed to Jerusalem to meet with Solomon. She tested his wisdom by using riddles and contests which Solomon was easily able to decipher. She said to him, "Everything I heard in my country about your achievements and wisdom is true." Before leaving she gave him "nine thousand pounds of gold and great quantities of spices and precious jewels." (*1Kings 10:10*)

The Message says: *A good reputation is better than a fat bank account.* Then adds, *Your death date tells more than your birthdate.* Your reputation tells, "who's on first."

Big Inning Baseball Quote #4:

Play long enough and people will know who you are:

"I want people to see me play at 50 years old and say, 'look what God has done with this weak man.' "

---Julio Franco---
Braves, First Base (46 in 2005)

Diamond Lesson #5

See Ball, Hit Ball

Our work as God's servants gets validated —or not—in the details.
2 Corinthians 6:4 (The Message)

Pete Rose, the owner of 4,256 Major League hits, once said that the process of hitting could be boiled down to, "See the ball, hit the ball." Perhaps Rose was guilty of oversimplification. Some folks say that hitting a baseball, at the Major League level, is the single most difficult task to perform in sports.

Consider this. A 90 mph fastball should reach the batter in 0.4 seconds. Consequently the hitter has about 0.1 of a second to recognize the pitch, discern where it is headed and get his bat started. While he is taking the luxury of that whole tenth-of-a-second to decide, the pitch will already have traveled about a third of the distance to home plate.

Often when a hitter is on a hot streak you will hear him say he is seeing the ball well. It really means he is 100% focused on the pitch, recognizing it quickly and getting the fat part of the bat on it often. He has to execute both parts of the equation. It ain't always easy. But, when you break down the art of hitting to its basic components Pete Rose was right. It's simply, "See the ball, hit the ball."

Just as a batter can be distracted, so can we when we are not focusing on the details. Famous Architect Frank Lloyd Wright used as a premise in his work, "God is in the details." That's what our scripture lesson today says. God is interested in all the details of our work and our play. It is by accomplishing the small stuff that we are able to tackle the big stuff.

The batter must see the ball well to hit it. In order to understand the whole picture we must see the small parts of the puzzle. Then, God will reveal the rest to us. Sometimes this requires patience. In our anxiousness we may not see all of the details. We may jump to conclusions and make erroneous decisions. Committing too early or too late invites failure.

In John 14:6 Jesus says, *I am the way, the truth, and the life. No one comes to the Father except through me.* That's pretty clear. If we want to get past the small stuff we must see that. Then, the rest will unfold in the way God planned.

Big Inning Baseball Quote #5:

A classic example of seeing it and hitting it:

"He had the greatest eyes and wrists of any hitter I ever saw."

---Ewell Blackwell—
on Ted Williams

Diamond Lesson #6

Grand Slam

Reaching into his bag and taking out a stone, David slung it and struck Goliath on the forehead. The stone sank in his forehead and the giant fell facedown on the ground.
1 Samuel 17:49

The Grand Slam! A home run with the bases loaded. Is there any more exciting play in baseball? Is there any greater feeling than to swing, watch the ball sail out of the ballpark, and start that jog around the bases as three teammates score in front of you?

One Grand Slam is nice, but how about doing it twice in one game? Incredibly, Fernando Tatis hit two "Slams" in the same inning in 1999 for the St. Louis Cardinals. Only one other player in the National League had hit two slammers in a game before and that was a remarkable story because he was a pitcher, the only moundsman ever to accomplish that.

The Sporting News Archives tell the story: "It was the 4th inning of the Braves-Giants game. The Braves had the bases loaded, two outs, and Tony Cloninger who had already hit one slam was facing lefty Ray Sadecki." When, Sadecki tried to zip a fastball past Cloninger he sliced it to right center field where Willie Mays ran to the fence and watched it sail over. A first and maybe a last. A pitcher hits two slams in one game!

The Grandest Slam in the Old Testament involved a little shepherd boy named David and a nine-foot tall giant, Goliath. The big bully was terrorizing the Israelites. When David brought lunch to his brothers they were cowering in the mountains with the rest of the troops, too afraid of Goliath to venture out.

David was unafraid. Unarmed, except for a slingshot and three smooth rocks, the little guy headed to the valley to face the fully armed giant. His brothers yelled, "David, are you crazy? Come back here."

It must have been quite a sight. This little shepherd boy looking up at this big, tall giant. The troops on both sides of the valley were looking down from their mountain perches as the two combatants approached each other.

When Goliath saw little David he laughed figuring this was some kind of a joke. Who, in his right mind, would think this little guy had any kind of a chance against that big bazooka? It would be the giant's last opportunity to laugh. It was David who had the last laugh as he slung the rock into Goliath's forehead and the giant slammed to the ground, never to rise again. David had accomplished an astounding Grand Slam.

We often face Giants in our lives in the form of multi-faceted problems. Sometimes they seem impossible to overcome. Then we must remember that God is able to handle any problem, small or giant-sized.

Like Tony Cloninger who accomplished the impossible for a pitcher, with God's assistance we become capable of grand-slamming even the giant-sized problems.

Then as we lift up our prayers for help we see not a giant-sized problem, but a giant-sized God ready to help us.

Big Inning Baseball Quote #6:

Talk about slamming a baseball:

"When Neil Armstrong first set foot on the moon, he and all the space scientists were puzzled by an unidentifiable white object. I knew immediately what it was. That was a home run ball hit off me in 1937 by Jimmie Foxx."

---Lefty Gomez---
Yankees pitcher, 1930-43

Diamond Lesson #7

Batting Average

Then Jesus told them, "I assure you, if you have faith and don't doubt, you can do things like this and much more.   Matthew 21:21

Batting average is the staple of baseball statistics for a hitter. It shows the consistency with which a batter does his job. A .300 hitter is considered to have had a good year. That average probably won't win the batting title, but it is an accepted standard of achievement because nobody hits .400 anymore. If a hitter bats .300, which puts him ahead of a majority of the batters, he still fails to get a hit seven out of every 10 at bats.

The most amazing hitter, when considering batting average, was Detroit outfielder Ty Cobb, who played in the American League from 1905-1928. Some people called him the "meanest man who ever played baseball." Cobb said, "I never could stand losing. Second place didn't interest me. I had a fire in my belly."

The Georgia Peach led the AL in batting average 12 times. He hit over .400 three times and had a .300 or better average for 23 years. In his career he had 4,189 base hits surpassed only by Pete Rose's 4,256 years later. Just before he broke Cobb's record Rose said, "When I get the record, all it will make me is the player with the most hits. I'm also the player with the most at bats and the most outs. I never said I was a greater player than Ty Cobb."

He may have played like the meanest man in baseball, but many years later in an interview with sportswriter Al Stump, Cobb said he had only loved two men in his life---Jesus Christ and his father, Professor W. H. Cobb.

One morning as Jesus was on his way back to the city He was hungry and saw a fig tree in the distance. When He went up to the tree He found only leaves, no figs. Then, He got angry. "May you never bear fruit again," He said. The tree immediately withered. His disciples were amazed at this.

Jesus was angry at a tree that gave false signals. It had leaves, but no fruit. What good was that tree to hungry travelers if it only had fruit on occasion. On that day it was of no benefit to Jesus and his disciples. By causing the tree to wither He demonstrated the power of God. He wanted his disciples to get the message that God's power was available to them and it could right the wrong things they encountered.

Jesus told the disciples if they had faith and didn't doubt, they would be able to perform acts like the one they had just witnessed. Confident Christians, keeping the faith will hit for a high batting average in life. Passionate belief or as Ty Cobb would say, "a fire in the belly" will overcome the obstacles to excellence.

Big Inning Baseball Quote #7:

One way to look at this batting average thing:

"If a guy hits .300 every year what does he have to look forward to? I always tried to stay around .190, with three or four RBI and I tried to get them all in September. That way I would always have something to talk about during the winter."

-Bob Uecker-
Catcher, Broadcaster

Diamond Lesson #8

Highlight Film Catch

His Master replied, "Well done thy good and faithful servant!   Matthew 25:21

When a player makes a spectacular play it is labeled a highlight film catch because it is one that will show up in a film of the team's season. One of the all-time most phenomenal catches in Major League Baseball occurred in the 1954 World Series. Those who saw it in person or on film are still scratching their heads and wondering how Willie Mays pulled it off.

The Cleveland Indians had set a new record with an impressive 111 wins during the regular season. With a pitching staff of Bob Lemon, Early Wynn, Mike Garcia and Bob Feller, the Indians were heavily favored over the New York Giants as the series got underway at the Polo Grounds.

Game One entered the eighth inning tied at 2-2. When Larry Doby walked and Al Rosen reached on an infield hit, the stage was set for the Indians power hitter Vic Wertz to break the tie. On a two-strike pitch Wertz got into it and drilled a screaming, long line drive to deep centerfield. Giants centerfielder Willie Mays was off at the crack of the bat. With his back to home plate, running full speed as he hit the warning track Mays reached up and caught the ball at about the 400 foot mark. Then, in one motion he stopped on a dime, whirled around and fired a strike to the infield preventing Doby from scoring.

The "Say Hey" Kid's miraculous catch kept the Indians off the board. Then, in the bottom of the 10th inning, with two men on base, pinch-hitter Dusty Rhodes hit a blooper down the right field line that only traveled 260 feet, but settled into the first row of the stands for a game winning homer.

Jesus told the parable of the master who went away on a long trip. Before he left he called three trusted servants in and assigned them different responsibilities. The one he gave five talents to doubled them in his absence and gave back ten talents. Likewise, the man who received two talents doubled those and returned four. The master complimented them. The third servant did nothing to increase what he had been entrusted with. Instead he went and hid it in the backyard and returned it, unimproved to the Master thereby incurring his wrath.

"The test of their service was not how much they earned, but how hard they tried. The first two servants each used his ability fully and earned one hundred percent return." They went all out and never gave up until the play was completed. Now their work has been highlighted in the scriptures down through the centuries.

Sometimes we can also make an impossible play, one that we will look back on as one of the highlights of a lifetime, a one-of-a-kind accomplishment. It will happen when we stay the course and visualize success instead of considering the odds of failing. Faith is a powerful tool in the arsenal of the believer.

Big Inning Baseball Quote #8:

Saving runs is as important as scoring them.

"Defense is baseball's visible poetry and its invisible virtue."

---Thomas Boswell---
"Why, Begins on Opening Day, 1984"

Diamond Lesson #9

Bench Jockey

He who guards his mouth and his tongue keeps himself from calamity. Proverbs 21:23

Bench jockeying is an art unto itself. The bench jockeys are the ones on the bench with the most "mouth." These guys needle opposing players, managers, and especially take exception to umpiring decisions. But, there is a limit…especially where the umpire is concerned.

Los Angeles Dodger reliever Eric Gagne was introduced to a bench jockeying rule while he was on the disabled list in 2005. The Dodger closer was made aware, by umpire Bill Hohn, of Official Baseball Rule # 3:17 which states: *Players on the disabled list are permitted to participate in pregame activity and sit on the bench during a game, but must not take part in any activity such as warming up a pitcher, bench jockeying, etc.*

Out for 15 days with a sprained right elbow ligament, Gagne would now be out for 17 days after receiving a two-day suspension for violating the bench jockeying part of that rule. Apparently Gagne thought he could call balls and strikes better from the bench than the umpire behind the plate and was tossed out of the game and banished to the clubhouse for heckling. Gagne said he was unaware he was violating the rules, but the umpire verified that ignorance of a rule is not a justifiable defense.

Over the years there have been some true masters of bench jockeyship in baseball. Some of the most active have included Billy Martin, Earl Weaver, Leo "the Lip" Durocher, and Lou Pinella. Bench jockeying even contributed to one of the most controversial home runs in history. In 1932, the Chicago Cubs bench jockeys were

41

giving Babe Ruth a good riding. This prompted the Babe, so legend has it, to turn and point to the centerfield fence indicating that was where he would hit the baseball in order to shut up the bench jockeys. He did. They did. That's according to legend.

More frequently than not a bench jockey's heckling comes back to haunt him. King Solomon referred to this kind of a problem in our scripture from *Proverbs*. The purpose of his instructions was to enable the reader to apply divine wisdom to daily life.

Solomon knew that our speech is the true test of our wisdom.

The key to guarding our speech lies in controlling one of the smallest parts of the body…the tongue. James points out (Chapter 3) that we put bits into the mouths of horses to control them, a ship's rudder can turn a large ocean-going vessel, and a small spark can start a forest fire. Likewise the tongue can "ruin the entire course of your life"

God's Little Instruction Book sums it up well: "Men are like fish. Neither would get into trouble if they kept their mouths shut."

Big Inning Baseball Quote #9:

Bench Jockey type of logic:

"Bob Gibson is the luckiest pitcher I ever saw. He always pitches when the other team doesn't score any runs."

---Tim McCarver---
former catcher and TV color man

Diamond Lesson #10

Middle Relief

For there is a time for every purpose and for every work.   Ecclesiastes 3:17b

Some jobs are boring, but necessary. On every team every player has to make a contribution to have a successful season. Perhaps, one of the least celebrated roles in baseball today is that of middle reliever who is not praised or appreciated enough, but is necessary.

The starting pitchers and closers get the glory. But, in an age where a complete game is a rarity, the work of the middle reliever is very important. The Boston Red Sox and St. Louis Cardinals were the pennant winners and World Series opponents in 2004. During the regular season Red Sox and Cardinal hurlers totaled only 4 complete games. Curt Schilling had 3 CGs en route to a 21-6 record and Pedro Martinez, 16-9, had one CG. The Cardinals Matt Morris, 15-10, recorded 3 CGs and Chris Carpenter, 15-5, had one complete game.

If it weren't for the Red Sox' relievers Alan Embree, Mike Myers, Ramiro Mendoza and Curt Lescanic, who appeared in a combined 155 games, and the Cards' middlemen, Cal Eldred, Steve Kline, and Kiko Calero, 160 games, these teams would not have been playing in late October. Hats off to the middle relievers, the unsung heroes in pitching.

Our daily lives are often filled with boring and seemingly menial, unimportant tasks. Often these are jobs that won't get done if we don't take the initiative and do them ourselves. No glory, just necessary.

King Solomon, the wisest of all kings, in searching for meaning in life questioned the importance of these humdrum tasks. He concluded in Ecclesiastes, *I've had a good look at what God has given us to do---busywork, mostly. True, God made everything beautiful in itself and in its time---but He's left us in the dark, so we can never know what God is up to, whether He's coming or going. (The Message)*

I'm reminded of the parable in Matthew in which Jesus says, "You have been faithful in few things, now you'll be able to oversee many things." That's why we have this busy work to do, so we may receive a bigger reward. It's like the Middle Reliever, who goes about his business and performs well. The end result is he will be able to join his teammates in the winning celebration, thanks to his effort in performing his assigned role.

Big Inning Baseball Quote #10:

Pitchers learn certain things if they last long enough.

"The oldest pitcher acquires confidence in his ball club. He doesn't try to do it all himself."

---Burleigh Grimes---
Major League Pitcher, 1916-1934
died at age of 92 in 1985

Diamond Lesson #11

The Sweep

They shouted, "A sword for the Lord and for Gideon!" While each man held his position around the camp, all the Midianites ran, crying out as they fled.
Judges 7:22-23

You are headed into the ballpark and you see fans carrying brooms with them as they go through the turnstiles. You're thinking, "Well that's nice these folks are going to sweep up their peanut shells before they go home, so they won't leave a mess around their seats." Wrong! The brooms are a warning to the opponents and a reminder to the home team. A win today and the home team gets a sweep. This can only occur if one team has won all the preceding games in the series. By winning the final game they take all of them and are deemed to have swept their opponents.

The worst time to get swept is in the World Series. When your team is four games from being crowned World Champs it is an embarrassment to get swept. That happened to the St. Louis Cardinals in the 2004 Series, the first one they had played in 15 years. The sweep was sweet for the Boston Red Sox, who won their first World Series since 1918 when Babe Ruth still pitched for them.

In 111 years (thru 2014) of playing the World Series there have been 20 sweeps. The first sweep came in 1907 as the Cubs, embarrassing losers the year before to the cross-town rival White Sox, shutout Detroit and held 20-year old batting champ Ty Cobb to a .200 average.

47

The team involved in the most sweeps has been the New York Yankees. They have swept their opponent eight times. The pin-stripers have lost all four games without a win in only three World Series.

When God chose Gideon to lead his army in battle against the Midianites He instructed him every step of the way. After the Israelite army had been reduced to a mere 300 men, God had their opponent right where He wanted them.

The Midianites were a fierce group of people who would raid opposing villages and take all the harvested crops and leave the place in shambles. They were camped in a valley and covered the countryside like locusts. But God had chosen the right team to get the sweep.

At a prearranged signal all the Israelites on one side of the camp blew their trumpets, broke glass jars, and gave a shout. The Midianites were in such a panic they began killing each other and fleeing, in complete disarray, to other cities. The Israelites had swept the Midianites.

When God grants the victory, it's huge. He empowers his people to pull off a sweep.

Big Inning Baseball Quote #11:

Sweeping certainly beats getting swept.

"The way things are going for me, if I'd buy a pumpkin farm they would cancel Halloween."

---Billy Gardner---
Manager, Twins, Royals 1981-87

Diamond Lesson #12

Bring the Heat

You will be thrown immediately into a blazing furnace. Then what god will be able to rescue you from my hand? Daniel 3:15

Flame throwers! Dominators! Guys who can bring the heat. These are the pitchers who can really fire the fastball. Radar guns consistently clock them in the mid-90's and even, on occasion, topping 100 mph.

You'll find them listed in the Hall of Fame. Sandy Koufax. Don Drysdale. Nolan Ryan. Bob Gibson. Some other heat-bringers include Roger Clemens who once struck out 20 batters in a game and Randy Johnson, who was inducted into the 2015 Hall of Fame class and once whiffed 19 in a game.

Those are pitchers who can afford to take a "blow-it-by-the-hitter-mentality." Yet, Koufax, who fanned 382 hitters one season (the most by a lefty) said, "I became a good pitcher when I stopped trying to make batters miss the ball and started trying to make them hit it."

Often the other pitches these "flame-throwers" have in their assortment will make hitters look foolish because the batter always has to expect the fastball and adjust to the breaking or off-speed pitch. Often that adjustment is made way too late and a weak, ineffective swing results. Yes, it helps to be able to really bring the heat because it disrupts everything for the hitter by keeping him off balance. To get a hit off one of these dominating pitchers shows that you've arrived as a hitter.

Daniel and his friends, Shadrach, Meshach, and Abednego, faced some heat of a different nature…real heat…killer heat. These young men had been taken from their homes in Judah and forced into service of King Nebuchadnezzar.

Instead of clamming up or curling up in a shell these guys made a difference. They excelled in all they did and made a big impression on the king—such a big impression he promoted them.

Feeling good about himself King Nebuchadnezzar constructed a 90-foot tall statue thinking he could have the whole kingdom bow down to this idol and thereby centralize worship. However, Daniel and his running mates refused and this infuriated the king.

So, he had them thrown into a fiery furnace. Talk about bringing the heat! They turned it up seven times hotter than usual. It was so hot that the flames leaped out and killed the soldiers who were throwing them into the furnace. Certainly this would provide an intimidating example for all those who dared to oppose the king's edicts!

But, Nebuchadnezzar underestimated the power of the one true God. Not only did they survive the fire, not even a hair on their heads was singed, nor were their clothes even scorched. Oh well, even bringing the heat against God's servants won't work. We are protected by His divine power.

Big Inning Baseball Quote #12

There are some things you can't apply heat to.

"Trying to throw a fastball by Hank Aaron is like trying to sneak the sunrise past the rooster."

--Curt Simmons—
Phillies Pitcher

Diamond Lesson #13

Ejected

Jesus went straight to the Temple and threw out everyone who had set up shop, buying and selling. He kicked over the tables of loan sharks and the stalls of dove merchants.   Matthew 21:12-13 (The Message)

Bobby Cox, was named Manager of the Year seven times. The Atlanta Braves finished in first place 14 consecutive times under his leadership. But Bobby holds one dubious record. He is the only manager or player ever to be ejected from two World Series games. Of the twenty-two ejections in World Series history only Cox has been bounced twice.

In the 1992 World Series against Toronto, Cox was ejected for arguing a check-swing call. That's one he can live with. His ejection in the '96 Series against the Yankees is a different matter. According to Baseball Almanac (http//baseball-almanac.com), trailing three games to two, the Braves faced elimination at Yankee Stadium.

They were behind 3-1 when Marquis Grissom reached on a hit and tried to steal second. He was called out despite television replays that showed he was clearly safe. An infuriated Grissom charged umpire Terry Tata and nearly bumped him. Cox came out to defend his player and dispute the call. On his way back to the dugout the highly incensed Braves skipper was still yelling back at the umpire and that's when he entered the record books for most times tossed out of a World Series game.

Arguments have always been a part of baseball. Seems there's often a difference of opinion between umps and players/managers. Orioles manager Earl Weaver always put on a good show when he argued with an umpire. He would turn the bill of his cap around so he could really get in the ump's face. Invariably an ejection would follow.

Mike Martin, in his early days of coaching Florida State University, was a creative objector to umpiring decisions. Once, to display his disgust with a call at first base, he simply pulled the base out of the ground and tossed it into right field. Then he was tossed out of the game by an unappreciative umpire.

Maybe anger is the wrong response in the case of those who are ejected from baseball games, but there are times in our lives when showing anger is appropriate. Jesus demonstrates such a time in Matthew 21: 12-13.

When Jesus entered the temple and saw the merchants selling their wares he became incensed and drove them out. This wasn't a temper tantrum. It was a justified action because the merchants, called moneychangers in some versions, were making it too crowded for people to worship in an appropriate manner.

In addition, according to the *NLT*, they would take advantage of visitors who had come a long distance to worship and didn't know the international exchange rate of their currency for temple coins. Likewise they gouged these folks on the price of sacrificial animals.

Such a practice angered Jesus into action. He ejected them from the temple.

Big Inning Baseball Quote #13:

A creative way to view ejections:

"I feel greatly honored to have a ballpark named after me, especially since I've been thrown out of so many."

---Casey Stengel---
on the Casey Stengel Plaza outside Shea Stadium.

Diamond Lesson #14

Home Run Hitters Drive Cadillacs

I can do all things through Christ who strengthens me.   Philippians 4:13

As the old anonymous saying goes; "Singles hitters drive Fords and Home Run hitters drive Cadillacs." Since Babe Ruth popularized the Home Run in the 1920's— a time of fast living, flappers, and fascination with the increasing speed of automobiles— baseball fans have been attracted to the long ball. There's something magical about watching a ball leave the bat and sail high and far, ending up in the stands or over a fence.

Ruth became known as the Sultan of Swat after he was the first batter to hit 30 home runs in a season, then the first to hit 40, then 50, and finally his record of 60 stood for 34 years until broken by Roger Maris in 1961.

When it comes to the longest recorded home run there seems to be a difference of opinion. At one time the Guinness World Book of Records said that honor belonged to a Mickey Mantle. On September 10, 1960, the Mick hit a ball completely out of Tiger Stadium in Detroit. Years after the fact, in reconstructing the scene and the landing area, it was determined that Mantle's blast traveled 643 feet. Still years later that one was disputed and the longest homer was attributed to Babe Ruth at 575 feet in 1921. Still, both of those guys could, to use a very old baseball term, "knock the cover off the ball."

It used to be that a batter would take off running after hitting a shot and only slow into a home run trot after the ball cleared the fence. To do otherwise would be considered showing up the pitcher. However, later some hitters led by the Giants Barry Bonds, who now holds the single season record of 73 homers, tend to stand at home plate and admire the drive, then take a walking start on the trip around the bases. That used to be considered showing up the pitcher and might warrant a bean ball next time up.

Major League umpire Randy Harvey had an interesting observation about the new approach. "Barry Bonds. I'll tell you what, if he hit a home run off Gibson or Drysdale and stood and admired it, they would knock that earring out of his ear the next time up."

It takes a certain amount of strength to hit a home run, but not necessarily Superman strength. Timing and bat speed contribute even more to the majestic flight of a home run. Likewise our strength comes from the Lord. When we do things in His time and at His speed He gives us the power tools we need to do the job.

Sometimes in the daily grind it seems the frustrations and failures we face just wear us out. We feel our strength waning and get a little discouraged because the roadblocks seem more numerous than the paths around them. In those times the apostle Paul encourages us to call on the Lord for the strength to get us through.

Paul wrote those encouraging words to the church at Philippi when he was in a place rife with discouragement. He was in prison. Seems strange that one who was a prisoner would have to encourage those who were free. Paul said he had learned to be content in whatever situation he was in. So, his body might have been in prison, but his mind was not.

Our problems can imprison us. But we are empowered by Paul's words that remind us we can do all things through Christ who strengthens us. When we draw on the Lord's strength our lives will stand out like a shiny new Cadillac in the midst of a bunch of jalopies.

Big Inning Baseball Quote #14:

No doubt about the automobile this guy drove:

"So what! I had a better year. How many home runs did he hit?"

---Babe Ruth---
responding to reporter's comments
that he was making more money than
President Herbert Hoover.

Diamond Lesson #15

Solo Shot

Immediately the fire of the Lord flashed down from heaven and burned up the young bull, the wood, the stones, and the dust. It even licked up all the water in the ditch. When the people saw it, they fell on their faces and cried out, "The Lord is God. The Lord is God." **1 Kings 18: 38-39**

A solo shot is a home run with nobody on the bases. One of the early and more famous solo shots was hit by Frank "Home Run" Baker. They called him "Home Run" Baker although he never hit more than 12 homers in a season. Yet he led the league three consecutive years in four-baggers. Playing in the "dead ball era," Baker, the Philadelphia Athletics third baseman from 1908-1922, built up quite a reputation as a long ball hitter. He actually earned the nickname in the World Series of 1911.

The New York Giants, managed by John J. McGraw, had a couple of brilliant pitchers in Christy Mathewson and Rube Marquard. Coming into the series they had collected 50 wins during the regular season. Mathewson and the Giants won the Series opener. The next day in game two, Marquard hooked up in a pitcher's duel with Eddie Plank. In the 6th inning he made a "poor pitch" which there was "no excuse for" according to an article ghost-written in Mathewson's name the next day. Baker who had powerful arms and wrists drove the ball over the right field wall and the A's won the game 3-1.

Back in New York the next day Mathewson, the author, would return to being Mathewson the pitcher and it would be his turn to face Baker. This time, on a 2-1 count, it was Matty who made a poor pitch with the same result. He later described the pitch as "a curve that hit more of the plate than I intended" and Baker hit the ball into right field stands to tie the game and 1-1. When the A's went on to win in 11 innings Baker was forever after dubbed "Home Run" Baker. Years later when asked how many home runs he thought he would hit with a "lively ball" instead of the one they played with in the dead ball era Baker said, "Probably fifty. The year I hit 12, I also hit the right field fence at Shibe Park thirty-eight times."

Elijah was called on to hit a "solo shot." God's prophet was competing against 450 prophets of Baal. The country was experiencing a horrible drought when the Lord told him to present himself to King Ahab and inform him that He would send rain.

There was one condition. To prove who the one true God was, Elijah demanded that all of Baal's prophets join him and the people of Israel on Mount Carmel. There they would call on their own god and the true God would send fire from heaven. Then it would rain.

With all the people watching they prepared two bulls and put each one on a separate altar. Then Elijah allowed the prophets of Baal to go first. They prayed, sang, danced, and pleaded. Nothing happened. Elijah even mocked them saying, "Maybe he is asleep yell louder." Still nothing.

Elijah prepared his bull, dug a trench around the altar, and completely drenched the bull with four large jars of water three times. The water overflowed the altar and filled the trench. When Elijah called on God He sent fire from heaven and it consumed the bull and dried up all the water even that in the trench. Afterward a rainstorm drenched the country as a result of Elijah's solo shot.

Big Inning Baseball Quote #15:

Seems like solo shots weren't the only four-baggers hit off these guys:

"The fans like to see home runs and we have assembled a pitching staff for their enjoyment."

> **---Clark Griffith---**
> **Owner, Washington Senators**

Diamond Lesson #16

Pinch Hitter

If any of your Israelite relatives go bankrupt and are forced to sell some inherited land, then a close relative, a kinsman redeemer may buy it back for them.

Leviticus 25:25

It may be one of the most difficult jobs in baseball. You're sitting on the bench for eight or nine innings, watching the game unfold before your eyes. You're comfortable, but your muscles, that were loosened up during batting practice, have now stiffened up. Your team is trailing by a run, there are two outs but you have a couple of men in scoring position. Then, you hear the manager call your name. The whole game is on the line. All the work the other players have done all afternoon will now succeed or fail as a result of what you are able to do as a pinch-hitter.

When looking at some of the all-time best in the pinch-hitting department names like Lenny Harris (804 ph Abs -7 teams), Gates Brown of Detroit (414 ph at bats), Greg Gross (591 ph at bats-3 teams),

Lenny Harris (212 pinch-hits) stands out. Other prominent pinch-hitters include, Willie McCovey, Ron Northey, Rich Reese, all with 3 ph Grand Slams. Not exactly household names.

One player who became a household name on the basis of one pinch-hit was Cookie Lavagetto. At the age of 34 the Dodger reserve was completing his 10th and last season in 1947. He had only batted 69 times during the season. He was an unlikely hero as the drama unfolded in Game 4 of the World Series with Brooklyn trailing the Yankees, 2-1.

Sitting in his familiar spot on the bench, Lavagetto was watching New York hurler Bill Bevens set the Dodgers down, and it appeared the American Leaguers would go up by three games because Bevens was pitching a no-hitter. However, his control was not sterling, as he had walked eight batters going into the ninth inning. Still, if he could retire the Dodgers hitless one more time Bevens would record the first no-hitter in World Series history.

In the ninth Bevens, with one out, walked Carl Furillo who was replaced by pinch runner Al Gionfriddo. Pinch-hitter Pete Reiser, worked the count to 3-1, and was issued a free pass, Bevens' 10th walk of the game. The no-hitter was still intact, until manager Burt Shotton pinch-hit little-used Lavagetto for Eddie Stanky. After a swinging strike Lavagetto dug in and lashed out at the next pitch driving a screaming liner to right field. By the time Tommy Henrich ran it down and sent it to the infield Gionfriddo and pinch-runner Eddie Miksis had crossed home plate. Pinch-hitter Cookie Lavagetto had spoiled the no-hitter and won the game.

In Old Testament times the kinsman-redeemer was a pinch hitter— a relative who members of the family could turn to for help to save the game. When the family possessions were in danger of being lost, the kinsman-redeemer would redeem them. He would buy back family land sold during a crisis or lost due to the death of a family member, and would provide an heir for a dead brother and care for relatives in times of trouble.

In one of the most romantic of Old Testament stories, found in the book of Ruth, wealthy landowner Boaz acted as a kinsman-redeemer. He not only bought the land that the widow Naomi was forced to sell and returned it to her, but he fell in love with her widowed daughter-in-law Ruth. When he married her he was playing the role of a

kinsman-redeemer and pinch-hitter for the deceased family member.

Big Inning Baseball Quote #16

Don't use this guy as a pinch-hitter:

"The hitter asks the owner to give him a big raise so he can go somewhere he's never

been and the owner says, 'You mean third base?' "

---Henny Youngman---
Comedian

Diamond Lesson #17

In the Gap

He is a voice shouting in the wilderness: Prepare a pathway for the Lord's coming! Make a straight road for Him. Matthew 3:3

"It's a gap shot."

"That was a gapper."

"He'll be looking for something he can drive. There's a big gap in left center."

Those are all descriptions that a play-by-play announcer could use to describe a hit to the outfield that travels into an open area between the leftfielder and centerfielder or between the rightfielder and centerfielder. The gap, also called the alley, is an area in which a hitter looks to drive the ball if he gets the pitch he can turn on.

Hitting the ball into the gap usually results in extra bases, frequently a double, sometimes a triple. With men on base it usually means at least one RBI. The outfielders try to hustle over and cut off a ball that is headed into the gap before it reaches the fence so they can hold the batter to a single.

Pitchers must have a gap mentality as well. At a crucial point in the game, with men on base, the guessing game between hurler and hitter is accelerated. While the batter looks to drive a pitch into the gap, the pitcher looks for a grounder, a harmless popup or even better a strikeout.

Location is the key. Can the pitcher ride a pitch in on the fists or get enough zip on a high fastball that the batter will get under it too much. Or can he stay low in the zone and get a ground out. It's all part of baseball's on-going chess game pitting the thrower against the swinger with "the gap" looming large in the strategy.

66

John the Baptist filled a gap between the Old Testament prophets and Jesus. He realized he was simply a forerunner. Sure, he was a little bit weird in terms of the clothes he wore (camel hair with a leather belt) and his food (locusts and honey). But the message he preached got people's attention.

John didn't mince words. He came right at his audience confronting them, warning them, and imploring them to obey God, to repent and turn from their ways. He let them know he was standing in the gap to announce the coming of One who was by far greater than he was.

John was a role player. His preaching was dynamic. When others told Him that Jesus was usurping his role and baptizing more people than he was, John said, "He is far greater than I am. I'm not worthy to be His slave."

There are going to be gaps in life that each of us needs to fill. We have a role to play, a job to do. When God sends opportunities our way we need to be ready to hit a game winning shot in the gap.

Big Inning Baseball Quote #17:

Obviously The Gap was more than a retail store to this hitter:

"I came to the Braves on business and I intended to see that business was good as long as

I could."

---Henry Aaron---
Home Run King

Diamond Lesson #18

Setup

In my Father's house are many rooms; if it were not so I would have told you. I am going there to prepare a place for you.   *John 14:2*

Most of the time the setup man does not get a win. He seldom gets a save. In fact, most of the time he plays second fiddle to the starting pitcher or the closer. His role is important even though he is kind of the offensive lineman of baseball. Not a whole lot of attention gets paid to him unless he blows a lead and ends up being the losing pitcher.

To recognize the important contribution a setup man or even a middle innings reliever makes to preserve a win, a new statistic was created in 1986. It is called the "hold." A pitcher can be credited with a hold if he enters the game with a lead of no more than three runs and maintains the lead for at least one inning.

As the game of baseball has evolved into one of specialists, the specific role of the setup man is to try to pitch a flawless inning or two and turn the game over to the closer in the ninth inning to preserve the win and get all the post-game high-fives as he walks to the dugout. He can get a "hold" for doing that. In fact, more than one pitcher can get a "hold' in the same game.

In 18 years in the Big Leagues up through the 2008 season, Mike Timlin pitched in 1,085 games. That total included only 4 starts and three of those came during his first season, 1991, with Toronto. Eventually he found his niche as a setup man.

In their championship season of 2004, it was a familiar sight to Red Sox fans to see Timlin, the 6'4", 210 pound Texan, his baseball pants stopping at the knees, come trotting in from the bullpen in the eighth inning. His 76 innings compiled in 76 games netted five wins, but more importantly he was able to preserve the lead and turn it over to closer Keith Foulke, who won five games and successfully preserved 32 other wins for Boston.

In the Gospel of John, Jesus talks about setting it up for us to enjoy the fruits of victorious living. In one of the few scriptures that refers to eternal life Jesus points out that your future is as safe, even though it cannot be presently seen, as your trust in Him is. You have to place your trust in Him to set it up for you.

Jesus promises that He will go ahead and prepare a place for us. It will be in His Father's house. We don't have to worry about there being room for us because Jesus says, *There are many rooms in my Father's home and I am going to prepare a place for you. If this were not so, I would tell you plainly. When everything is ready I will come and get you.*

All we have to do is trust Him. We don't have to fear death, life or eternity because Jesus is preparing for us to spend eternity with Him. He will have it all set up for us.

Big Inning Baseball Quote #18:

A solid pitching staff sets up a winning formula:

"You give us the pitching some of these other clubs have and no one could touch us, but

God has a way of not arranging that because it is not as much fun."

---Sparky Anderson---
manager

Diamond Lesson #19

The Cycle

After a long time their master returned from his trip and called them to give an account of how they had used his money. The servant to whom he had entrusted five bags of gold said, 'Sir, you gave me five bags of gold to invest and I have doubled the amount. *Matthew 25:19-20*

Hitting for the cycle is a phenomenal feat. It means the batter has hit a single, a double, a triple and a home run in the same game. The hits don't have to occur in that order to hit for the cycle, but if they do the batter has accomplished a "natural" cycle.

Since the first cycle was achieved in 1882 by Curt Foley of the Buffalo Bisons, 306 players have hit for the cycle in the ensuing 133 years, an average of less than one per year.

Hitting for a natural cycle is even more rare. Only thirteen players have accomplished that in a Major League game. Those twelve include Bill Collins (Braves-1910); Tony Lazzeri (Yankees-1932); Bob Fothergill (Tigers-1926); Charlie Gehringer (Tigers-1939); Leon Culberson (Red Sox-1943); Bob Watson (Red Sox-1979); Billy Williams (Cubs-1966); Ken Boyer (Cardinals-1964); John Mabry (Cardinals-1996); Tim Foli (Expos-1976); Brad Wilkerson (Expos-2003), Jose Valentin (White Sox-2000) and Gary Matthews Jr. (Rangers-2006).

Two teams—the Padres and Marlins never have had a player hit for the cycle. The Giants have had the most with 25, followed by Pirates with 23, then the Redsox and Cardinals with 20.

Sluggers who never did hit for the cycle include Babe Ruth, Hank Aaron, Mark McGuire, Barry Bonds, and Willie Mays. Twelve major leaguers have hit for the cycle on two occasions. The champion cycle hitter has to be Irish Bob Meusel of the Yankees. He is the only player in baseball history to accomplish the feat three times (1921, '22 & '28).

Today's scripture lesson features another remarkable feat. A man was going away on vacation and he surveyed his lineup before leaving. He called together three servants. He entrusted each of them with some money to invest for him while he was gone.

When he returned he found that the first servant had done a lot with his at bat. He had basically hit for the cycle by returning the five bags of gold his master had given him and five more as well. The master was pleased and said "well-done thy good and faithful servant."

The man who had received two bags of gold returned it with two more. This also pleased his master. Both of these men had achieved something special in their master's sight.

The man who had received one bag of gold went and hid it in the ground, so it wouldn't get stolen. The master was displeased with his lack of creativity. He took that one bag and gave it to the servant with ten bags of gold.

Each man had a chance to excel, just like a batter who hits for the cycle. Yet, only two of them succeeded. To achieve excellence sometimes you need to take a risk. When you do, you might just hit for the cycle.

Big Inning Baseball Quote #19:

Instead of the cycle maybe he's talking about re-cycle:

"During my 18 years I came to bat almost 10,000 times. I struck out about 1,700 times and walked maybe 1,800 times. You figure a ballplayer will average about 500 times at bat a season. That means I played seven years in the Major Leagues without ever hitting the ball."

---Mickey Mantle---

Diamond Lesson #20

Curveball

So, you can see that we were not preaching with any deceit or impure purposes or trickery.   1 Thessalonians 2:3

Sometimes life just throws you a curveball. That's a statement you've probably heard before. More than likely this baseball terminology is something you have experienced. The fact is a curveball can be very difficult for a batter to hit, especially if he is set for a fastball. A curveball is a major weapon in most pitchers arsenal.

Many times we hear that a hitter will look for the fastball and adjust to the curveball. This is the case especially when facing a hard throwing pitcher whose fastball registers in the mid-to-upper 90's.

Here's the difficulty with that strategy. A big league curveball can move as much as 17 ½ inches from a straight line by the time it crosses home plate. To make it even more difficult most of the curving takes place in the last 15 feet. Generally, it only takes the ball about $1/6^{th}$ of a second to travel that last one-quarter of the trip. Since it takes a batter about $1/5^{th}$ of a second to swing the bat, you can see he has to start the swing before much of the curving has started.

Add to this is the fact that a curve ball drops sharply and curves to the left (for right-hand pitchers, opposite for southpaws) and the degree of difficulty in hitting a curveball is exceptional. It takes instant pitch recognition and quick reaction to hit a good curveball.

While a curveball is hard to hit, if that's all a pitcher threw, pitch after pitch then a major league hitter would adjust to it. Some of the great curveball throwers of all time

75

had overpowering fastballs that set up their curveball pitch to look like a World Class offering. Guys like Sandy Koufax, Nolan Ryan and Bob Gibson were prime examples.

Often in life we have difficulty dealing with the curveball that comes our way because we are looking for something else. Paul wrote to the church at Thessalonica, where he visited on his second and third missionary journeys, a warning not to let the false teachers throw them a curveball.

He pointed out that there were people out there who would try to fool them. These leaders would attempt to distort what Paul was saying. The tactic they used was to tell the Thessalonians that Paul, Timothy, and Silas were pretending to be their friends in order to get money from them.

Paul pointed out that he had been imprisoned at Philippi before coming to Thessalonica, but that had not dissuaded him. Fear of imprisonment never kept Paul from preaching the Good News. His preaching was based on the purest of motives. He wanted to please God, not people because God is the one who "examines the motives" of their hearts.

The Thessalonians didn't have to fear that Paul would throw them a curveball.

Big Inning Baseball Quote #20:

Sounds like there's a curveball in there somewhere:

"I use my single windup, my double windup, my triple windup, my hesitation windup, my no windup. I also use my step-n-pitch-it, my submariner, my sidearmer, and my bat dodger. A man's got to do what he's got to do."

---Satchel Page---

Diamond Lesson #21

Hit and Run

Again the Israelites did what was evil in the Lord's sight. So the Lord handed them over to the Midianites for seven years. The Midianites were so cruel that the Israelites fled to the mountains where they made hiding places for themselves in caves and dens.
Judges 6:1-2

Timing is the key to successful execution of the hit and run play in baseball. Generally, a manager will call for a hit and run when there is a runner on first base with less than two outs. As the pitcher releases the ball the runner starts for second as if he has received the steal sign.

Then

it is up to the batter. He is called on to hit the ball on the ground, preferably to the spot just vacated by either the second baseman or shortstop who has headed to cover second base. The batter doesn't want to hit the ball in the air because the runner will have to retreat to first base.

The hit and run is a classic strategy for advancing a runner. Even if the batter hits the ball directly to a fielder, they may avoid a double play because the runner had started with the pitch. When it works properly the ball is hit in the hole for a single and the runner advances to third base. The worst-case scenario is a line drive to a fielder that results in the runner being caught in limbo and causing a costly double play.

Wee Willie Keeler was probably the consummate hit and run player because of his tremendous bat control. One of the smallest players ever to reach the major leagues, he stood only 5'4 ½ inches tall and weighed 140 pounds. In 1892, at the age of 21, he broke into the Big Leagues with the New York Giants. Keeler played 19 years and his batting average was .341. His famous saying, which speaks to the reason he was a good man to have at the plate when the manager flashed the hit and run sign was: "I keep my eyes clear and I hit 'em where they ain't." That's the key to executing the hit and run.

The Midianites were a hit and run group. A fierce desert people, descended from Abraham's second wife Keturah, they would watch a village while the people worked hard to plant their crops. When the crops were harvested the Midianites would hit the village and steal the harvest.

God used the Midianites to punish the Israelites for their disobedience. Years earlier the Israelites battled the Midianites and almost destroyed them. Contrary to God's instructions they did not completely eradicate them. Now, the Midianites had grown back to full strength.

When the *Israelites did what was evil in the Lord's sight, He handed them over to the Midianites for seven years.* The Israelites had hit rock bottom. Unfortunately that's what it often takes for people to straighten their lives out. When, they are stripped of everything and have no place to turn, they look to God.

The Israelites had been hit by the Midianites and they ran to the mountains. Now they would turn back to God and admit that they were unable to help themselves.

God provided the means for them to, once again, defeat the Midianites.

Big Inning Baseball Quote #21:

This guy was the best to have at the plate to pull off a hit-and-run:

"George Brett could get wood on an aspirin."

--Jim Frey—

Diamond Lesson #22

Stealing

Thou shalt not steal.   Exodus 20:15

Baseball is the only sport where stealing is allowed. A stolen base occurs when the base runner safely reaches the next base as the pitcher is delivering the ball to home plate.

Stolen bases are meticulously recorded. Not just the number of bases stolen, but the caught-stealing numbers are also kept.

According to Wikipedia, the on-line encyclopedia, for a time in the 19th century a runner was given a stolen base if he advanced an extra base on a base hit. For example, if the runner on first base went to third base on a single he would be given a stolen base for advancing from second to third. The modern rules for base stealing erasing that scorekeeping oddity went into effect in 1898.

You've heard it said by radio announcers after a stolen base occurs, "He stole that base off the pitcher." That happens when the runner gets such a big lead before the pitcher delivers the pitch that it is impossible for the catcher to throw him out. Good timing is essential in stealing a base. The runner has to leave base early enough to beat the catcher's throw, but not so early that he gets picked off base by the pitcher.

Anyone daring enough to steal home must have impeccable timing. Ty Cobb, who popularized the art of base stealing in the early 1900's, still holds the career record for steals of home with 54. Only 11 players have stolen home twice in a game. The last time that was accomplished in the American League was 1958 by Vic Power of the Indians. No one has stolen home twice in a game in the National League since 1927.

Cobb said baseball changed after Babe Ruth started hitting home runs. The stolen base was no longer appreciated. He felt that stealing bases required more talent and anyone could hit a home run. One day in 1925, to prove the point, he told writers he was going to swing for the fences for two consecutive games. In the first game he went 6 for 6 with three homers and set a new record with 16 total bases in a game. The next day he hit two more homers and recorded 9 consecutive hits for the two games. After that he went back to playing his style of baseball which included lots of stolen bases.

Stealing may be okay in baseball, but not elsewhere. One of the 10 Commandments that God gave to Moses on Mount Sinai specifically said, "Thou shalt not steal." These Commandments were given to the Israelites so they would know how to conduct themselves. They had just escaped from Egypt where there were many different gods.

Each of the Egyptian gods represented a different aspect of life. It could be very confusing, trying to figure out which god to worship. So the Egyptians worshipped many gods to try to maximize the blessings they received.

God showed the Israelites His true nature by giving them these laws. By obeying them they could lead a life of holiness. The Ten Commandments represent a plan for living. They were simple, common sense laws for respecting each other and getting along in a community.

Among the important rules these included were to honor their parents, not commit murder or adultery, lie, or use God's name falsely. And one of those rules that is very important in life, but not in baseball, said "Thou shalt not steal."

Big Inning Baseball Quote #22:

The reason base stealing is important:

"A good base stealer should make the whole infield jumpy. Whether you steal or not,

you're changing the rhythm of the game. If the pitcher is concerned about you, he isn't

 concentrating enough on the batter.

---Joe Morgan---
Hall of Fame, 2B

Diamond Lesson #23

Baltimore Chop

Why, O Lord, do you stand far off? Why do you hide yourself in times of trouble?
Psalm 10: 1

It's a helpless feeling.   The winning run is on third base with two outs. You're the third baseman and the batter swings mightily and hits a Baltimore Chop. As you see the winning run running past you down the third base line all you can do is wait for the ball to come down and hope you have time to throw out the batter negating the run and preserving a tie score.

That's basically what a Baltimore Chop is. It is a ball that goes straight down after connecting with the bat, hits the ground, and bounces high in the air. The only option a fielder has is to wait for it to come down while positioning himself to make a very quick throw after he finally catches the ball.

Intentionally trying to hit a Baltimore Chop was a legitimate strategy during the Dead Ball era. From 1900 to 1920 the league leader in home runs had only 10 round trippers or fewer in 13 seasons. The ball was deader than it is nowadays, so a team had to manufacture runs any way it could. So, swinging down on the ball to achieve a big bounce that would allow runners to advance was a strategy that hitters with good bat control would use.

A pitching strategy to avoid the Baltimore Chop would be to keep the ball up in the strike zone since it is unlikely the hitter could get on top of a high pitch and hit it down. In current times, with batters swinging for the fences, most pitchers try to keep the ball low in the strike zone to induce ground balls. Batters taking a full swing at the ball are unlikely to hit a Baltimore Chop. Those occur accidentally nowadays.

The Psalmist was experiencing the same kind of a helpless feeling in Psalm 10 that a fielder waiting on the descent of a Baltimore Chop feels. We're not sure who the Psalmist was, but it was believed to be David because the 9th and 10th Psalms are frequently linked together and he wrote Psalms 9.

The frustration he was feeling came at a time when he needed God most, and He seemed most distant and unreachable. This happens in our lives sometimes. We just can't seem to get through to God. Injustice may be happening all around us and we just aren't getting any answers.

Even though the Psalmist was frustrated, he still knew that God was aware of every injustice that was being carried out. He wasn't complaining as much as he was beseeching God to hurry up with his aid. When we have this feeling, that's the time to step up the prayers. Let God know just what we are feeling. He hears every prayer.

The *NLT* says, "Why are we angry when the wicked prosper. Are we angry about the damage they are doing or just jealous of their success?" We just have to remember that the wicked will be punished because God hates evil deeds. "Wealth is only temporary. It is not necessarily a sign of God's approval on a person's life; nor is it a sign of God's disapproval. Don't let wealth become your obsession."

The Baltimore Chops in life will eventually settle in our gloves. We just have to be ready and remember it will come about in God's timing, not ours.

Big Inning Baseball Quote #23:

You'd be lucky to even get a Baltimore Chop off these guys:

"That's like asking if I'd rather be hung or go to the electric chair."

---Merv Rettenmund---

Baltimore OF, when asked if he would rather face Jim Palmer or Tom Seaver

Diamond Lesson #24

Earned Run Average

So, my dear brothers and sisters be strong and steady, always enthusiastic about the Lord's work, for you know that nothing you do for the Lord is ever useless.
1 Corinthians 15:58

In a time long, long ago, starting pitchers were routinely expected to pitch the whole game. The won-loss record of a pitcher was a good indicator of how effective he was. Then, relief pitching became fashionable after 1900. If a starting pitcher left early and the reliever got credit for the decision there was no way to measure what kind of a job the starter did in contributing to the victory or defeat.

Henry Chadwick, an early sportswriter and statistician (the man who invented the box score) created the earned run average to measure a pitcher's effectiveness. The ERA as it is called is the average of runs given up by a pitcher per nine innings. ERA=9 times the number of earned runs divided by the number of innings pitched.

To have an earned run average of less than 2.00 for a season is considered exceptional and has become rare in modern times especially for a starting pitcher. There are some dazzling exceptions like Bob Gibson's 1.12 ERA in 1968. During that season the St. Louis right-hander threw 13 shutouts. In a stretch of 92 innings he only allowed two earned runs. That record still stands as the lowest ERA for a full season. But, the next year Major League Baseball lowered the height of the pitching mound by 5 inches. Gibson still had 20 wins and a 2.18 ERA.

In 2000 Pedro Martinez of the Red Sox finished at 1.74 making him one of only two pitchers, who have led both the American and National leagues in ERA with sub-2.00 marks. In 1997 Pedro had a NL leading mark of 1.90 while pitching for Montreal.

Roger Clemens also led both leagues with sub-2.00 ERA recording a 1.93 mark with Boston (AL) in 1993 and 1.87 with Houston (NL) in 2005.

The ERA definitely says something positive about a pitcher's work and as a result Martinez was voted into the Hall of Fame in 2015.

A pitcher's earned run average keeps him from getting discouraged when he keeps pitching well, but doesn't have the victories to show for it.

The apostle Paul, in writing to the church at Corinth tried to encourage the Christians there not to weary in well-doing. Paul knew that it was easy to become apathetic about the Lord's work when the results were meager. He encouraged the Corinthians to always be enthusiastic about the work they were doing.

As Paul pointed out nothing we do in the Lord's name is useless because of the resurrection. God will bless all that we do and He has provided proof of that. Jesus won the ultimate victory for us. In 1 Corinthians 15:55 Paul says: "Death is swallowed up in victory. O, death where is your victory? O death, where is your sting?"

Things may seem to go wrong in life. Friends and relatives pass away. We keep trying to do all the right things but we don't feel like we are getting anywhere. Paul says there is a way to measure the effectiveness of what we do. Just like the pitcher with few wins could get discouraged if he didn't look at his low ERA, so we could get discouraged if we don't look at the cross.

When we enthusiastically do the things the Lord asks us to do our work is not useless. The salvation we have through the resurrection of Jesus authenticates all that we do in His name.

Big Inning Baseball Quote #24:

At least this requirement would help your earned run average:

"It was unbelievable in Chicago. You felt you had to pitch a shutout to tie."

---Rich Gossage---
on the hapless '76 Whitesox

Diamond Lesson #25

OBP

A voice of one calling in the desert, "Prepare the way for the Lord, make straight paths for Him."   Matthew 3:3

Some managers view on base percentage (OBP) as the most important statistic in gauging a player's value to the team. OBP is computed by taking the number of hits, walks, and hit-by-pitch that a player has and dividing it by his at bats, walks, hit-by-pitch, and sacrifice flies.

Obviously scoring runs is the name of the game in baseball. You can't win a game if you don't score runs. And getting men on base is the key to scoring runs. You can't rely on home runs for all of your runs.

That is not to say that home run hitters aren't good OBP guys. Take Ted Williams for example. "The Splendid Splinter" played 19 years and hit 521 home runs while batting .344 with a slugging percentage of .634. At the same time he had a career OBP of .481, a record unmatched in baseball. Williams lead the league 12 times in OBP. That's not only an American League record, but is tops in the majors.

Pitching to Williams wasn't much fun. Bobby Shantz pitched in the Major Leagues for 16 years. Shantz once said: "Did they tell me how to pitch to Ted Williams? Sure they did. It was great advice, very encouraging. They said he had no weaknesses, won't swing at a bad ball, has the best eyes in the business, and can kill you with one swing. He won't hit anything bad, but don't give him anything good."

Being in the field when Williams was batting wasn't much fun either. "I got a big charge out of seeing Ted Williams hit," said Rocky Bridges, then he added. "Once in awhile they let me try to field some of them, which sort of dimmed my enthusiasm."

Getting on base consistently sets the stage for the great hitters to excel. John the Baptist realized that he was a stage setter for the One who would cause great things to happen in this world.

John the Baptist played on the people's curiosity to accomplish his task. He got on base by preaching that One was coming who was greater than he. John looked kind of strange. He wore clothes made of camel hair and he ate locusts and wild honey. He loudly proclaimed that the people should get ready for a big event.

He got on people's case. He denounced the Pharisees and Sadducees who were coming to be baptized by calling them a "brood of snakes." He said they thought they could do anything they wanted because they were descendants of Abraham, then added: "That proves nothing. God can change these stones here into children of Abraham."

He was the "…voice shouting in the wilderness: 'Prepare a pathway for the Lord's coming!
Make a straight road for him!" John the Baptist wanted to make sure the people were ready for Jesus when He came.

Today we are preparing for His second coming. When Jesus comes we definitely want to be on base. When we are on base for the Lord, then Jesus will take our OBP to a higher level.

Big Inning Baseball Quote #25:

Guess that means this guy was on-base a lot:

"Mickey Mantle can hit just as good right handed as he can left handed. He's just naturally amphibian."

---Yogi Berra---

Diamond Lesson #26

Spring Training

You must be ready all the time, for the Son of Man will come when least expected.
Luke 12:40

Spring Training is many things to many people. To the young player trying to make the Big League team it can be a stressful time of trying to attract attention. For the established stars it is a more relaxing time of getting into shape for the long season and sharpening their skills. The managers look at it as a time of evaluating and projecting what kind of team they will have. The front office looks for trade opportunities and prospects. And the fans just enjoy watching a Major League game while basking in the beautiful springtime weather. No matter what your position or stake is in Spring Training, it is a time of preparation for the real thing, when all those numbers count…the Season.

According to the Baseball Almanac website, the first professional teams held Spring Training for a couple of weeks in their own home park before the season began. Originally major league teams played the early games against minor league teams, but this was discontinued in the early 1920's. Soon all of the teams decided to move to a warmer climate for this rounding-into-shape process and stretched it out to a month. Thus began the Grapefruit League, so named for teams training in Florida, and the Cactus League for those training out west, mostly in Arizona.

Over the years teams have trained in such diverse locations as French Lick, Indiana, and Catalina Island, California. Every team has moved around a bit. Some have settled on Spring Training sites that work well for their team and have just stayed there.

Longevity records for Spring Training locations are all Grapefruit League sites. In 2005, the Dodgers began their 56th consecutive year of Spring Training in Vero Beach, FL. The Phillies started their 58th year in Clearwater. But, the record for most years in one place goes to the Detroit Tigers, who have trained in Lakeland, FL for 69 consecutive years (thru 2015) dating back to 1946. During World War II they trained in Evansville, IN. Prior to that they were also in Lakeland from 1934-42. The Detroit Tigers, who have had the same name and hometown since 1901, have also been consistent in Spring Training spending 77 springs in the same location.

In a way our life on earth is merely Spring Training for the big game. When compared to eternity, the time we spend here is small. Jesus said that we must prepare for His return. We do that by trusting Him and learning how we should conduct our lives. We are polishing our game and getting ready just like the Big Leaguers do in Spring Training.

Jesus said that a homeowner who knew exactly when a burglar was going to break into his house could prevent it. But, the thief doesn't announce his arrival. Likewise we do not know the exact day and time of Christ's return.

In the meantime we are in Spring Training. We're preparing to be the best we can be. We're getting the fundamentals down right, so when it is time for the season, we'll be ready. We've been given the talent and the ability to perform the task God has set before us. Jesus said: "Much is required from those to whom much has been given and much more is required from those to whom much more is given. " God is watching to see how we play the game.

Big Inning Baseball Quote #26:

Is this guy going to be ready for Spring Training or what? :

"People ask me what I do in the winter when there's no baseball. I tell you what I do. I stare out the window and wait for spring."

---Rogers Hornsby---

Diamond Lesson #27

Pitcher's Best Friend

When the spirit of truth comes, He will guide you into all truth. He will not be presenting His own ideas; He will be telling you what He has heard. He will tell you about the future. John 16:13

For 23 years whenever a Baltimore Oriole pitcher was in a jam there was nothing he would like better than to see a ground ball heading in the direction of third base. That's where the "human vacuum cleaner" played. Brooks Robinson started 618 double plays from the hot corner.

The double play has been called the pitcher's best friend because it provides a quick way to get out of trouble. When you have a player of Robinson's ability with quick reflexes and sure-handed fielding skills, anything hit his way has a chance to turn into two outs. His fielding prowess was so renowned that Sparky Anderson once said Brooks could "throw his glove out on the field and it would start 10 double plays all by itself." Right-handed slugger Johnny Bench said he might switch to hitting left- handed against the Orioles just to keep the ball away from Robinson.

Five years after Robinson retired, a player by the name of Cal Ripken Jr. came along to play shortstop for the Orioles. Ripken broke the "unbreakable" record of Lou Gehrig by playing in 2,632 consecutive games from 1982-1998. During that time Ripken was involved in 1,565 double plays, a record at the time for American League shortstops. Together they totaled 2,183 double plays by two men and the AL record at each position.

The pitcher's best friend was a big factor in Baltimore baseball for 40 years.

At other positions Hall-of-Famer Nellie Fox (White Sox) holds the AL record for double plays at second base with 1,568. And of course most double play balls end in the glove of the first baseman. Mickey Vernon (Senators) has that AL record with 2,041.

Jesus revealed some startling news to His disciples. He would be going away and they wouldn't see Him any more. While they began to bombard Him with questions, He hastened to assure them that it was good that He was going because He would send a friend to help them. This friend, The Holy Spirit, would counsel and lead them. He would become their best friend.

Jesus knew what lay ahead for the disciples. Just as He would be persecuted and crucified.

He also knew the disciples would suffer persecution as would Christians for centuries to come. But, He knew the Holy Spirit would be their helper. The NLT Bible says, "Christ's presence on earth was limited to one place at a time. His leaving meant He could be present to the whole world through the Holy Spirit." When, Jesus became a human for the world's sake, he was limited to human attributes. He could not be omnipresent. Now, through the Holy Spirit He could work in everyone's life.

Through His death on the cross, Jesus made a personal relationship available to us. As believers we receive the power of the Holy Spirit. The Spirit helps us through "patient practice to discern right from wrong." The Spirit is a guiding force in our lives to the extent that we let Him be.

In Jesus and the Holy Spirit we have friends who start the double play of righteousness and salvation in our lives that is completed at first base with the Heavenly Father.

Big Inning Baseball Quote #27:

Seems like these guys started a nice trend that all pitchers appreciate:

"Making a Giant hit into a double,

words that are heavy with nothing

but trouble, 'Tinker to Evers to Chance.' "

---Franklin Pierce Adams---
NY newspaper columnist, 1910

Diamond Lesson #28

Tools of Ignorance

I saw that wisdom is better than folly just as light is better than darkness.
Ecclesiastes 2:13

Charlie Brown is standing on the pitcher's mound ready to start the game when his catcher comes out to go over the signals he will be flashing during the game. The catcher says, "One finger will mean just *try* to get it over the plate. Two fingers will mean *try not* to throw it over the backstop. And three fingers will mean we'll all be glad when the season's over." Then, the catcher turns and heads back to home plate and Charlie Brown says, "Catchers are weird."

Yes, they are weird. So weird in fact the catcher's equipment is referred to as the "tools of ignorance." In 1876, Harvard's Fred Thayer adapted a fencing mask into a catcher's mask for his college team and soon all catchers were wearing them. In 1886, Detroit Tiger catcher Charles Bennett's wife made him a chest pad that became the forerunner to the catcher's chest protector. Giants Catcher Roger Bresnahan was the first to wear shin guards in 1907 although he took some ribbing when he showed up at home plate wearing the converted hockey goalie protection that covered his legs from his knees to the top of his shoes.

Those three items plus the catcher's mitt are the tools that baseball's most rugged players use in a game. Catchers often receive as many as 150 pitches in a game with many of those reaching speeds of 90 mph and more. When you add all the pre-game catches and those between inning warm up pitches and when a relief pitcher comes in, a catcher may catch as many as 300 balls on game day. Catchers have to crouch to play the game. They get knocked down by sliding base runners, nicked by foul balls, and have to chase wild pitches. No wonder Muddy Ruel once concluded, on a hot day while getting ready to catch Walter Johnson's fastballs that he was putting on the "tools of ignorance."

Is choosing to become a catcher in baseball a display of wisdom or folly? A wise man named King Solomon once pursued the meaning of both, to determine what was really important in life. He surmised that it is best to learn if the action you are contemplating is wise or foolish before you act.

The Believer's Bible Commentary says: "His (Solomon's) general conclusion was that wisdom is better than folly to the same degree that light excels darkness. The wise man walks in the light and can see the dangers in the way. The fool, on the other hand, gropes along in the darkness and falls into every ditch and trap."

We are constantly making life choices that affect many areas of our lives. Sometimes it all seems hopeless because things don't work out right. Solomon was dealing with that in Ecclesiastes 1 and voices his frustration. He says that it has all been done before, and whatever he does is just history repeating itself. "There is nothing new under the sun. It's all like chasing the wind. It's meaningless."

Solomon set out to get all he could in as many areas as possible to overcome this helpless feeling. He accumulated real estate, gold and silver, many wives, but none of it satisfied him. Only wisdom survived. It was better to be smart than ignorant. It doesn't matter how much we have or what we wear. We can don the tools of ignorance, but in the end gaining wisdom and acting wisely is what counts.

Big Inning Baseball Quote #28:

Could you explain that again, Yogi? :

"Congratulations. I knew the record would stand until it was broken."

---Yogi Berra---

(congratulating Johnny Bench on breaking his record for most homers by a catcher)

Diamond Lesson #29

Stuff

So I tell you don't worry about everyday life---whether you have enough food, drink and clothes. Doesn't life consist of more than food and clothing?   Matthew 6:25-26

Two-seam fastball. Four-Seamer. Sinker. Slider. Curve. Screwball. Knuckler. Changeup. Palmball. Splitter. There is an endless array of pitches in baseball these days. How many pitches does a pitcher need to be successful? How much stuff does he have to possess to make it to the Big Leagues?

There's no set answer. It depends on the pitcher. Most of them have at least three pitches…a breaking ball, fastball, and changeup. A pitcher who has good stuff is one who gets good movement on all of his pitches. Any pitch that comes in straight goes out straight…usually out of the ballpark. A ball that is moving a little when it reaches home plate either minimizes the bat's impact or fools the batter for a strike.

The great Dizzy Dean, who won 120 games in one five-year stretch, dismissed the myth of having lots of different pitches to win games: Old Diz said, "The dumber a pitcher is the better. When he gets smart and begins to experiment with a lot of different pitches he's in trouble. All I ever had was a fastball, a curve, and a changeup and I did pretty good." Dizzy was so adept at keeping batters off balance he would, at times, ask the hitter, "Son, what pitch would you like to miss?"

Cy Young won 511 games in 22 years of pitching. That's why the award for the best pitcher in the American and National League is named after him. Young said that one day he tried to show just how much stuff he had. "I thought I had to show all my stuff and I almost tore the boards off the grandstand with my fastball." He then pointed out the key to his success. "Control is what kept me in the Big Leagues." Having stuff doesn't matter if you can't control it.

Sometimes we think we must have a lot of stuff to enjoy life. Whether it is the fanciest car, a wardrobe full of the latest fashions, newest state-of-the-art electronic equipment or the biggest, most impressive house; stuff consumes us. The material things in life have great appeal and their importance can easily become distorted.

None of those things is necessary for us to carry on in life. Sure, they can make life a little more fun or easier. Stuff can also complicate life. If we get caught up in having the latest and the greatest we add unnecessary stress to our lives.

Jesus says in Matthew 6 that we miss the real meaning in life if we center our lives around stuff. In so doing we imply that God isn't looking out for us. We're saying God doesn't want us to have the best of everything. That is not true! God loves us and likes for us to be happy. He knows that stuff is not what will make us happy.

Jesus points out that we have the basics because of God's goodness. He simplifies it by giving the example of the birds: Thanks to their Creator they have enough to eat and drink. What about the Lilies…how beautiful are they? This is not because of anything they have done. God has dressed them out like that.

If we get caught up in worrying about stuff our lives will pass by and someday we will realize we had all the stuff we needed. We just didn't use it meaningfully and because of that we have missed the main purpose in life.
It's like the pitcher who focuses on having lots of stuff and fails to develop the control he needs to be successful.

Big Inning Baseball Quote #29:

Sounds like the right stuff…unless the umpire examines the ball:

"If K-Y Jelly went off the market, the whole California Angels pitching staff would be out of baseball."

---Bill Lee---
Red Sox pitcher in 70's

Diamond Lesson #30

Slugging Percentage

This was their song. " Saul has killed his thousands and David his ten thousands."
1 Samuel 18:7

The slugging percentage is calculated by dividing the number of official at-bats a player has into the number of hits while assigning 1 point for a single, two for a double, three for a triple and four for a home run. Babe Ruth holds the highest career slugging percentage with a .690 mark.

With that figure in mind how does a slugging percentage over 3000 for one game sound? Incredible? Yes, it was. On May 9, 1999, Marshall McDougall of Florida State University set a record that will probably never be equaled.

Marshall started the game off calmly enough with a single at College Park where the Seminoles were playing then ACC opponent Maryland. What the Seminole second baseman accomplished in successive plate appearances was phenomenal. In six consecutive at bats McDougall hit six home runs.

When the historic day was over here is what McDougall had accomplished. Seven for seven at the plate, and new records with six home runs, 25 total bases, 16 RBI and seven runs scored. A 1.000 batting average for the day and 3,571% slugging. Oh yeah, the Seminoles won, 26-2.

Some accomplishments are too incredible to be overlooked. David was a natural. After he had slain the giant, Goliath, David was rewarded by King Saul by being given the rank of a commander in the Army.

Saul had been a powerful and successful warrior. When David came along the people of Israel realized as the saying goes, "we ain't seen nothing yet." David continued to succeed in every assignment he was given and his popularity increased with every success. He was setting new records.

Saul was relegated to the role of a singles hitter. It was not the position he wanted to be in. He was the king, but David was getting all the glory.

When David and his troops returned to town after a victory the women would line the streets to greet them with songs. They sang that Saul had done some remarkable things by killing thousands of the enemy, but what David had done was exceptional. His slugging percentage had reached the ten thousands.

Don't settle for the ordinary in your life because through God you can achieve the extraordinary.

Big Inning Baseball Quote #30:

This guy was always out there slugging:

"I coulda hit a .400 lifetime average easy. But, I woulda had to hit them singles. The people were paying to see me hit home runs."

                    ---Babe Ruth---
                    1920-34, Yankees

Diamond Lesson #31

Field of Dreams

I will pour out my spirit on all people…your old men will dream dreams, your young men will see visions.   Joel 2:28

"If you build it, he will come!"

Ray Kinsella was hearing things. He had some differences that had never been reconciled with his deceased father. He missed him and wanted one more chance to see him. The one thing they had in common was a love of baseball. And now he was hearing this ghostly voice telling him if he built a baseball field on his farm in Iowa that his Dad would come there to play a game.

Ray, played by Kevin Costner in the movie "Field of Dreams," started out on a venture of faith. He went to Boston to see a controversial writer, Terrence Mann, played by James Earl Jones to find out the meaning of the voices. Here's what Mann tells him:

> "The one constant through all the years, Ray, has been baseball.
> America has rolled by like an army of steamrollers. It's been
> erased like a blackboard, rebuilt, and erased again. But baseball
> has marked the time. This field, this game, is a part our past, Ray.
> It reminds us of all that once was good, and that could be again.
> Oh people will come, Ray. People will most definitely come."

As an exercise in faith Ray Kinsella begins to build his baseball field of dreams. And they come. No one but those who believe can see the ghostly ball players. The ghosts of Shoeless Joe Jackson and the other players disgraced in the 1919 "Black Sox" baseball scandal come back for one more game.

And yes, there is Ray's dad. One more time he and Ray have a game of catch, just like the old days of Ray's childhood. As they toss the ball back and forth the troubles of the past rollaway. Baseball is the mending and healing salve they needed. Ray's faith has been rewarded.

In a way every baseball field is a Field of Dreams. Every kid who has ever played a game on a home-grown backyard field or sandlot, or high school field has dreamed dreams of someday being a baseball player and making it to the Major Leagues.

In Joel 2: 28, God is telling the people of Israel that their dreams will be fulfilled. They have been through captivity, a plague of locusts, and at times, they have lost hope that God is watching over them. God tells them not to fear that He will pour out his Spirit on His people.

He says that the old men will dream dreams and the young men will see visions of how things could be and He will fulfill these. He will bring about these things and bless His people, but they must have faith. They have to believe that His word is true and His promise will be honored. Just as only the ones who believed could see the ghostly players who returned to the Field of Dreams, the people of Israel were told that they must be believers and must keep the faith to have their dreams realized.

They must believe what wonderful things God would bring about in their lives. "I will cause wonders in the heavens and on earth," He told His people. God doesn't want to destroy. He wants to heal and save. We must believe He can. Then, He will. As the advertisement for the movie says: "If you believe the impossible, the incredible can come true."

Big Inning Baseball Quote #31:

If you're going to dream, be sure and dream big:

"Kids are always chasing rainbows, but baseball is a world where you can catch them."

---Johnny Vander Meer---
Reds famous double no-hit
pitcher, 1937-49

Diamond Lesson #32

Wild Pitch

But, Caleb tried to encourage the people as they stood before Moses. "Let's go at once and take the land," he said. "We can certainly conquer it." Numbers 13:30

July 15, 1884 was either the best day or the worst day of young Mike Corcoran's life. Call it the best day if you consider breaking into the Major Leagues and pitching a complete game a good thing. But, it could be considered bad if you look at his performance for the Chicago White Stockings. He gave up 16 hits while setting a pitching debut record with 5 wild pitches. It was the only game he ever pitched in the Big Leagues.

Corcoran's ignominy pales compared to what happened to poor Rick Ankiel. The promising lefthander from Ft. Pierce, FL, made his post-season debut as a surprise starter for the St. Louis Cardinals in the 2000 playoffs. The 19-year old with the 95-mph fastball had won 11 games in helping the Cards reach the postseason. No one expected him to start that first game against Atlanta. Ankiel probably wishes he hadn't.

His five wild pitches in the fourth inning were the most by a pitcher in the 20th century. Ankiel ended up throwing nine wild pitches in four innings of work. Any one who watched the game had to feel sorry for the youngster who just couldn't make his pitches go where he wanted. The psychological impact of those wild pitches cut short a promising pitching career. Eventually, Ankiel decided to give up pitching.

Even though a wild pitch can put a team in a bind and lead to defeat, some pitchers can shake it off. Walter Johnson once threw four wild pitches in an inning. In fact the "Big Train" threw 154 wild pitches in his career and hit 205 batters. He won 417 games in 21 seasons. The adverse affects of a wild pitch can be overcome, but they can be devastating as well. Nobody likes to make a wild pitch, however, some recover more quickly than others from this mistake.

God had brought the Israelites from bondage in Egypt to the brink of the Promised Land. All they had to do was take it. Being overly cautious they decided to send men out to scout the land. Twelve were chosen to check it out.

What the men found was a land blessed by God. It was a very fertile, beautiful land. We read in Numbers 13:23 "They cut down a cluster of grapes so large it took two of them to carry it on a pole between them." It was truly, as promised, a land "flowing with milk and honey."

For forty days they explored the land before returning to report to Moses and their people. They reported that it was truly a magnificent land, but…"the people living there are powerful and the cities and towns are fortified and very large."

Caleb spoke up and said, "We can certainly conquer them." The others started exaggerating a little saying, "They are stronger than we are…the land will swallow up any who go to live there." The clincher was: "We even saw giants there…We felt like grasshoppers next to them and that's what we looked like to them."

In comparison to those tall tales, Caleb's confident minority report sounded hollow and more hopeful than factual. It seemed as if Caleb was making a wild pitch. So, they rejected Caleb's plea, thereby incurring God's wrath and being forced to wander in the wilderness for forty years. Caleb survived his wild pitch to succeed another day. Only he and Joshua from that entire nation lived to enter the Promised Land.

Big Inning Baseball Quote #32:

Sometimes a wild pitch has a purpose.

"It helps if the hitter thinks you are a little crazy."

-Nolan Ryan-
Hall of Fame Pitcher

Diamond Lesson #33

Ruthian Clout

O Lord, our Lord how majestic is your name in all the earth! You have set your glory above the heavens.   Psalm 8:1-2

The ball leaves the bat and all eyes look up! Its flight keeps going up into the stratosphere until it lands high in the stands behind the outfield or disappears from view, going out of the ball park. This majestic home run is called a Ruthian clout. The only question on this kind of a blast is how far it will go.

This type of home run is named after the "Babe" because that's the way he used to hit them. Although Babe Ruth's records continue to be broken, his uniqueness and impact on the game of baseball will never be equaled. As famous sports columnist Red Smith once said: "It wasn't just that he hit more home runs than anybody else, he hit them better, higher, farther, with more theatrical timing and a more flamboyant flourish."

When Ruth was traded to the Yankees by the Red Sox in 1920, it was a move from which Boston has never recovered. The Red Sox average record for the first 14 seasons without the Babe was 54-95. Meanwhile the Babe and his clouts had taken the Big Apple by storm. His popularity knew no boundaries. Babe endorsed everything from shave cream to underwear.

In those days the Yankees played their games at the Polo Grounds. According to the book "Babe Ruth: His Life and Time" published by *Publications International* on the 100th Anniversary of his birthday: "Of the first 16 homers Ruth hit at the Polo Grounds in 1920 all reached the second deck or left the park completely."

This phenomenal start prompted W.O. McGeehan of the *New York Herald-Tribune* to write: "Each home run seems to possess an individuality and eccentricities of its own." Memories of Ruth's prodigious homers are preserved in photos, books, movies and those grainy old game films. Don't be surprised the next time you hear a radio or TV announcer say that the majestic home run just hit was a Ruthian Clout.

Majestic is a good way to describe God. As David writes in the 8th Psalm, the majesty of his name fills the earth. When we look at His creation and all His wonders it is easy to feel small and insignificant, but God doesn't want us to dwell on this. As the NLT Bible says: "Humility means proper respect for God, not self-deprecation."

Even though we are small, God has so much love for us that He made us just a little lower than Himself. That proves we are valuable. And if that wasn't enough Psalm 8:6-8 says, "You put us in charge of everything you made, giving us authority over all things---the sheep and the cattle and all the wild animals, the birds in the sky, the fish in the sea and everything that swims the ocean currents.

God created everything, and then He turned it over to us. We are in charge of the whole earth. That's a great responsibility. We are over all things, and we must take care of them. This means pets and plants and natural resources. Everything! What an awesome and majestic God. Only he could show that kind of trust with something so valuable. That's why we should take time to admire and respect the beauty of His creation. It is a unique accomplishment. Sportscasters called the Babe's Ruthian Clouts majestic. It's a term they borrowed from the Psalmist to describe the awesome one true God.

"O Lord, our Lord the majesty of your name fills the earth!

116

Big Inning Baseball Quote #33:

Obviously a Ruthian clout is no ordinary blast.

"No one hit home runs the way Babe did. They were something special. They were like homing pigeons. The ball would leave the bat, pause briefly, suddenly gain its bearings, then take off for the stands."

---Lefty Gomez---
Yankees, 1930-43

Diamond Lesson #34

Passed Ball

Then, the people began to murmur in disagreement because he had said, "I am the bread from heaven." They said, "This is Jesus, the son of Joseph. We know his father and mother. How can he say, "I came down from heaven."   John 6:41-42

In his classic book, *Baseball's 50 Greatest Games* sports-writing legend Bert Sugar writes: "The plight of the Brooklyn Dodgers in 1941 instigates the moral reflection that life is made up of smiles, sobs, and sniffles, with sniffles undoubtedly prevailing."   Those Dodger sniffles were caused by a famous passed ball.

A passed ball is a pitch that should be caught by the catcher, but is missed and allows a runner or runners to advance a base. If a runner scores on the passed ball that's bad. If the winning run scores on it that's terrible.

In 1941 the Dodgers made it to the World Series for the first time since 1920. Sugar says they did it with "a catalogue of store-boughts who had gone through the season hollering and whooping and kicking everybody out of the way." Over in the American League, "God was apparently back in His heaven and all was again right with the world as the New York Yankees reclaimed their rightful perch atop that league for the fifth time in six years," remarked Sugar.

Trailing two games to one, the Dodgers fell behind 3-2 in game four. Then, Pete Reiser hit a two-run homer and Hugh Casey came on to protect the one-run Dodger lead. In the 9th inning, with two outs and nobody on, the Yankees were down to their last hope. Tommy Heinrich was at the plate with a full count. Casey let fly with a hard slider that was headed out of the strike zone. Heinrich tried to check his swing, but couldn't.

118

Umpire Larry Goetz signaled strike three and the game was over, but the game wasn't over. Catcher Mickey Owen missed the ball and Heinrich was safely headed to first base running on a missed third strike---a passed ball. Before the Yankees could be retired, they scored four runs to win the game. The next day they won again leaving Dodger fans talking about the passed ball that cost them a World Series.

Centuries before Mickey Owens' unforgivable mistake, some unforgiving people in another place were talking about the strange occurrence in their hometown. Jesus, who they knew as a kid growing up working in his father Joseph's carpenter shop, had returned home. He attended services as usual and stood up to read the scriptures. The synagogue had served as a school for youth during the weekday and a place of worship on the Sabbath when Jesus lived there.

After reading the words of the prophet Isaiah. He said that the scriptures had been fulfilled that day. He was the one Isaiah was referring to. But, they knew full well Jesus was from Nazareth, not from heaven. "How can this be? Isn't this Jesus the carpenter's son? What kind of blasphemy is this? He always seemed like such a nice boy."

As Jesus continued to talk, He said that no man is a prophet in his own hometown. He didn't do any of the miracles they heard he had performed elsewhere. The crowd became angry. They chased him outside and were going to throw him over the cliff but He slipped away. The anger of the home crowd did not easily pass.

Big Inning Baseball Quote #34:

A player who never passed up a ball.

"When I was a kid, I used to ride my bike around in the winter with my glove hooked onto the handlebars. There was always snow around, but I wanted to be ready, just in case one of my friends had a ball."

---Bob Buhl---
Braves pitcher, 1953-62

Diamond Lesson #35

Around the Horn

Then, all three groups blew their horns and broke their jars. They held the blazing torches in their left hands.   *Judges 7:20*

Third to second to first. A 5-4-3 double play. That's the definition of around-the-horn. It is often a sharply hit ground ball that the third baseman fields cleanly, fires to the second baseman who steps on the base and relays it to the first baseman completing a double play. It's a quick way to get two outs. Pitchers love it.

More rare would be the situation in which there are runners on first and second. The third baseman is playing even with and close to the bag. A hot grounder is hit his way and he steps on third, throws to second and the relay to first gets three outs. A triple play! That's magical.

Brooks Robinson (Orioles) started the most double plays by a third baseman in his career to hold the major league record with 618. The NL record holder is Mike Schmidt (Phillies) with 450.

The record for hitting into double plays, (many of which were around-the-horn) a dubious honor, are held by two of baseball's all-time greats. Hank Aaron, who holds the coveted record for most home runs in a career, also has the NL record for hitting into double plays with 305. Cal Ripken Jr., who started the most consecutive games of anyone, has the AL record with 335. This is evidence that around-the-horn double plays can happen to anyone. With a runner on first and less than two outs, it's a sure thing that a pitcher's first thought is "around-the-horn-double play" when he gets a grounder to third base.

It's not known why they call it the horn…in the around-the-diamond double play. A Biblical hero named Gideon made good use of horns to win a big one for the Lord. When the Midianites were camped in the valley getting ready to attack the Israelites, God prepared a plan for Gideon to execute.

It consisted of using only 300 men to defeat the entire Midianite camp. Gideon wasn't so sure. His faith needed a little shot of courage. God allowed Gideon to slip into the Midianite camp unnoticed. While he was hanging around, he heard one of the guards talking to another about a dream he had.

"I had a dream that a loaf of barley bread came tumbling down into the Midianite camp. It hit a tent, turned it over, and knocked it flat." (Judges 7:13) Gideon interpreted that dream as sign of victory from the Lord."

Thus, in the middle of the night, when all was quiet in the valley, Gideon and his 300 men were up in the mountains surrounding the camp. On a pre-determined signal they broke their clay jars, held blazing torches in their left hands, and blew their rams horns. Simultaneously they shouted "A sword for Gideon and a sword for the Lord." The Midianites panicked, began fighting each other, running away, and were captured easily by Gideon's men. The noise from around the horns had sealed the victory.

Big Inning Baseball Quote #35:

A double play controls an inning very nicely.

"Baseball is the only sport I know that when you're on the offense, the other team

controls the ball."

---Ken "the Hawk" Harrelson---
former player, then a broadcaster

Diamond Lesson #36

Inside the Park Homer

May the Lord bless you and protect you. May the Lord smile on you and be gracious to you. May the Lord show you His favor and give you His peace. Numbers 6:24-26

A common explanation for a story that elicits only a few laughs or nods of acknowledgement is that it must be an "inside joke." It can only be understood and appreciated if you are familiar with or have first hand knowledge about the situation, i.e. you must be on the "inside" to know what's going on.

In baseball a home run that never leaves the ball park is an "inside the park homer." It triggers a flurry of activity, but is only appreciated by the team at bat and its supporters. Inside the park home runs are rare. They usually occur because of some freak happening like an outfielder falling down in pursuit of the ball; two fielders running into each other; or the ball taking a weird bounce off the fence.

During the last 50 years of the 20th century inside the park homers accounted for about one out of every 158 home runs. With smaller ballparks this number has dwindled. The record for the most inside the park-ers in a season has stood for a long time. In 1901, Sam "Wahoo" Crawford, of the Cincinnati Red Stockings had 12 homers that didn't leave the park. Ty Cobb (Tigers) holds the AL record with nine in 1909.

More rare is an inside the park grand slam homer. Honus Wagner (Pirates) holds the career mark with five. There have only been eight inside the park grand slams in all Major League games from 1990 to 2015. Roberto Clemente is the only player in baseball history to hit a walk-off (game-ending)inside the park grand slam homer (July 25, 1956).

Inside the park home runs provide some of the greatest thrills in baseball.

The Israelites had their own inside story that was just between them and God. It was a blessing. A blessing was their way of asking for divine favor. The ancient blessing found in Numbers 6 results from God's instruction to Moses that he have the priests, Aaron and his sons, bless the people with a special blessing. This blessing had five parts to it. According to the NLT Bible the blessing conveyed hope that God would:

(1) Bless and protect them

(2) Smile on them (and be pleased)

(3) Be gracious (merciful and compassionate)

(4) Show his favor toward them (give his approval)

(5) Give peace

This was an inside story. It was an agreement between God and Israel. In return for their being designated as His people God would keep those wonderful promises. He would bless them and prosper them. Sounds like a great deal. A real no-brainer. We wonder, with all this inside information, how the Israelites could ever get off-track. As long as they kept their focus on God and his promises they would be okay.

We know the rest of the story. We read how they arrived at the doorstep to the Promised Land and were afraid to go in. They forgot the inside story…the blessing from God that the priests had bestowed on them. Their fear blotted out God's promise to protect them and give them peace.

The inside story provides an advantage, but only when the information is acted on. An inside the park homer is not complete if the batter stops at third base. He must go all the way, just as the Israelites were required to go all the way with God's blessing.

Big Inning Baseball Quote #36:

An inside the park homer has its own special rewards including handshakes

(high-fives):

"I'm glad I don't play anymore. I could never learn all those handshakes."

---Phil Rizzuto---
former player, play-by-play announcer

Diamond Lesson #37

The Bullpen

Then, David died…he had reigned over Israel for forty years, …Solomon succeeded him as king…and he was firmly established on the throne.   *1 Kings 2:10-12*

As any baseball fan knows the bullpen is the area where the relief pitchers warm up with the anticipation of entering the game. A team's bullpen can be located down the foul line near the stands, in the corner or behind the outfield fence.

How this area came to be known as the bullpen has been greatly debated over the years. Here are some of the more popular opinions. Take your choice:

1. In the late 19th century if you arrived late to a game you would be directed to a standing room only area where the fans were packed in like cattle…hence it came to be called the bullpen.

2. Symbolically it represents an area where bulls were kept before going to the slaughter or into the arena at a bullfight. So, relief pitchers are kept there before entering the game.

3. Casey Stengel said it was called bullpen because managers got tired of relief pitchers "shooting the bull" in the dugout and sent them elsewhere so they wouldn't bother the team.

4. Another early theory was derived from the fact that many of the areas where pitchers warmed up were in front of the Bull Durham Tobacco sign.

Take your pick of name origins. It is certain in modern baseball with its scarcity of complete games, when you attend a ball game, you'll see the manager call to the bull pen for help when his starting pitcher falters.

David was king of Israel for 40 years. Waiting in the bullpen were two sons- Adonijah and Solomon-who wanted to become king when he died. Adonijah was David's fourth son. Since Amnon, Daniel, and Absalom were deceased, he was next in line to be king. It was well known that David favored Solomon, his son by Bathsheba.

When David was very old and confined to bed Adonijah decided to make himself king and bump Solomon out of contention. He took chariots and horses and fifty men along with army commander Joab and priest Abiathar to a spring where he offered sacrifices and proclaimed himself to be the new king.

Word got back to David through Bathsheba and the prophet Nathan and he became very angry. David called the priest, Zadok and told him to put Solomon on the king's personal mule, take him to another spring, and anoint him king over Israel.

After this had been done, they blew trumpets and shouted, "Long live King Solomon." When word reached Adonijah at his celebration, all the people deserted him like he had the plague. He even ran to Solomon, who was already on the throne, and bowed low, fearing he would be killed. Solomon told him to "go on home."

Solomon came out of the bullpen to take over, and he gained the reputation as the wisest of all Israel's kings.

Big Inning Baseball Quote #37

What is happening down in that bullpen?

"There's someone warming up in the Giants bullpen, but he's obscured by his number."

-Jerry Coleman-
Padres broadcaster,
former major league player

Diamond Lesson #38

Going, Going, Gone

During the night, the disciples were in their boat out in the middle of the lake and Jesus was alone on land. He saw that they were in serious trouble, rowing hard and struggling against the wind and waves. About 3 o' clock in the morning he came to them, walking on the water.   Mark 6:47-48

Many people have said that baseball is the best sport to listen to on radio. A primary reason for that is the colorful language employed by the baseball play-by-play guys. And of course the home run provides the opportunity for some real creativity on the part of the announcer.

In my 23 years of broadcasting FSU baseball my favorite home run call was to simply say, or perhaps shout would be a better description, "There's a drive to deep right field. It's going…going…gone."

There are many other distinctive home run calls that are associated with individual sportscasters. For example, Giants announcer Russ Hodges would say, "Bye, Bye Baby" when a Giant hit one out. Vin Scully, longtime voice of the Dodgers says, "Forget it" as the ball leaves the park.

According to www.baseball-almanac.com here are some of the other trademark home run calls of major league broadcasters:

- "Get up, get outta here, for (player's name)   Bob Uecker
- "It could be, it might be…home run   Harry Caray
- "Long gone"   Ernie Harwell
- "Swing and there it goes. Light tower, power"   Jerry Trupiano
- "Goodbye Dolly Gray"   Leo Durocher
- "Open the window Aunt Minnie, here it comes   Rosey Roswell
- "Kiss it goodbye"   Bob Prince
- "Holy Cow"   Phil Rizzuto

- "Long drive, way back, warning track wall,
    you can touch 'em all."   Greg Schulte

But, one of the most creative home run calls belongs to Dave Neihaus, voice of the Seattle Mariners. "Get out the rye bread and mustard Grandma cause it's Grand Salami time." That's a home run call that's hard to top.

The sixth chapter of Mark reports a feat that is impossible to duplicate, unless you are the Son of God. The disciples were still struggling to get a grip on just who Jesus was. He had just completed one of his great miracles by feeding a group of 5,000 with only five loaves of bread and two fish.

Now the crowd had left and the disciples got in the boat to head back across the lake and Jesus went up to into the hills to pray. Then a huge storm cropped up. They were in big trouble trying to row the boat against the wind and waves.

When Jesus saw their dilemma he came to them walking on water. This was at three a.m. You can imagine what their first reaction was, when in the midst of this major problem, they look out and think they see a ghost walking on the water. They probably figured they were "going, going, gone."

Jesus spoke to them saying, "It's all right. I am here. Do not be afraid." Then, he climbed in the boat and the wind stopped. They had been in deep trouble, but now the Master had rescued them. His presence calmed the storm and their fears.

That is a good lesson for all of us. The Master may seem to be far away, but He is watching over us. We don't have to handle these problems alone. The one who could feed 5,000 and walk on water is there for us as well.

Big Inning Baseball Quote #38:

A player who pitchers wished was going, going, gone:

"He was zero-for-twenty-one the first time I saw him. His first major league home run was off me and I'll never forgive myself. If I had only struck him out we might have gotten rid of Willie Mays forever."

--Warren Spahn---
Hall of Fame Pitcher, Braves

Diamond Lesson #39

Warming Up

However, no one knows the day or hour when these things will happen, not even the angels in heaven or the Son himself. Only the Father knows. And since you don't know when they will happen, stay alert and keep watch.   Mark 13:32-33

Warming up! It's what you do on a cold day. You sit in front of a fire with a cup of hot chocolate and it feels good to warm up. For a pitcher it doesn't have to be a cold day to require warming up. Even in 100 degree temperatures before the pitcher goes into a game his arm has to be loose. So he throws warm up pitches. Starting pitchers and relievers throw in the bullpen before they enter a game. During the game they also throw warm-up pitches from the pitcher's mound before the start of each inning. Getting his arm warm helps the pitcher gain flexibility and avoid injury.

Warm up time is a time for practicing the pitches that will be used. It doesn't matter how many pitches are in a pitchers arsenal the main thing is to be able to throw them for strikes. Sometimes during pre-game warm-ups, you'll hear a pitcher say he just "couldn't get loose." Or maybe he'll say "didn't have my good stuff in warm-ups." This means he is not getting his pitches to attain the movement they need.

Hardly any pitcher will call off a start because his pitches aren't working while he is warming up. Sometimes those pitches come around during the game with a real live batter at the plate. Conversely, a pitcher may feel great in warm-ups, have all his pitches working, and go out and get shelled in the game. Who knows? That's why they play the game!

In 1928, Paramount made a film called "Warming Up" starring Richard Dix and Jean Arthur. Dix was showing some amazing pitching accuracy at a local park where he entertained customers with these skills. Along comes Arthur, whose Dad just happens to own the "Green Sox" baseball team, and discovers him. The rest of that success and love story is history. A pitching career emanated from warming up.

When a relief pitcher gets the call to go into the game he needs to be warmed up and ready to go. Likewise we are told that our journey on earth is just a warm up for the real thing. It is a small amount of time compared to the time we will spend in eternity.

So we need to be warmed up and ready. Jesus said that even He didn't know the end time. Only God knows that time. When Jesus came to earth he took on human form and with those human characteristics, He, like you and I, did not know when it all ends.

We plan for the big events in our lives. We put great thought into choosing a mate, weddings, births, choice of college, careers, job changes, investments, buying a home, a car, a refrigerator, etc. Why wouldn't it make sense to plan for eternity?

Jesus says since only the Father knows that time, it would behoove us to "stay alert and keep watch." Jesus set a pattern for living that is pleasing to the Heavenly Father. Now He is in Heaven where we will be judged. On earth Jesus was warming up for His return to heaven. That journey now has a "been there done that" tag on it. From experience Jesus knows how hard it is for us to stay warmed up and ready to go. He encourages us to do the wise thing and be ready.

Big Inning Baseball Quote #39

If warm-ups are tough for the catcher of a knuckleball imagine a batter's dilemma:

"Trying to hit Phil Niekro is like trying to eat Jell-O with chopsticks."

---Bobby Murcer---
Yankees infielder

Diamond Lesson #40

Extra Bases

If a soldier demands that you carry his gear for a mile carry it two miles.
Matthew 5:41

Extra bases mean excitement. When a batter hits a double, triple, or a home run he is credited with an extra base hit. Everybody is in action when this happens. The outfielders give chase, the infielders cover their respective bases, off comes the catcher's mask (with men on base), and the pitcher even goes in motion. For example, Dodger great Carl Erskine once said, "I had pretty good success with Stan (Musial) by throwing him my best pitch and then backing up third." That's where the pitcher goes on an extra base hit to right or centerfield, unless the ball leaves the park.

Of course lots of pitchers spent time backing up third base when they pitched to Stan "the Man" who got his nickname when wearing out Brooklyn Dodger pitchers. The fans at Ebbetts Field would say, "here comes the man again" whenever Musial came to bat.

During his Big League career Musial lead the league in extra bases in seven seasons and finished in the top five 14 times. Musial's first hit in the majors was a double and his 3,000[th] hit was a double. Teammate Joe Garagiola once said: "He could have hit .300 with a fountain pen." And Hall of Fame pitcher Warren Spahn lamented, "Once Musial timed your fastball your infielders were in jeopardy."

During 22 seasons in the big leagues Musial had 1,377 extra bases. He was just behind the great Hank Aaron (Braves) with 1,477 and slightly ahead of another guy everybody knows about, Babe Ruth, who had 1,356. When it comes to extra bases Stan Musial, the Cardinal Hall of Famer, will long be remembered as one of the best.

Just as it takes doing something extra to get an extra base hit in baseball, Jesus calls on us as Christians to do something extra in our lives. In one of the more difficult commands to fulfill, Jesus instructs us in Matthew 5 about loving our enemies. This is a tough one!

Jesus said, "But, I say don't resist an evil person! If you are slapped on the right cheek, turn the other, too. If you are ordered into court and your shirt is taken from you, give your coat, too," (Mat 5:39-40, NLT). In fact, the Message translation says, "If someone sues for the shirt off your back, gift wrap your coat and make a present of it."

Then He added more difficulty in the instructions to the Jews who were being oppressed by the Romans and wanted revenge against them. They were told if a soldier makes you carry his gear for a mile, carry it for two miles. You can imagine how that was received. It's tough advice for us to follow because we naturally want to strike back when we have been wronged or offended.

Why did Jesus tell us to do these extra, difficult things? Probably because we are not to take the law into our own hands. God will ultimately right the wrongs, not us. Our role is to "pray for those who persecute you." It's not easy to give up what we feel are our rights and to "bite our tongue" when we would like to punch somebody's lights out.

If we go the extra mile we will reap the rewards just like a batter who hustles and takes the extra base.

Big Inning Baseball Quote #40

Extra base hits even get the play-by-play guys excited:

"That's the fourth extra base hit for the Padres—two doubles and a triple."

-Jerry Coleman-
Padres announcer

Diamond Lesson #41

Three Blind Mice

Since you call on a Father who judges each man's work impartially, live your lives as strangers here in reverent fear.   *1 Peter 1:17*

When I was growing up and went to the Macon Peaches (South Atlantic League) minor league games, they would play the theme from the kids song "Three Blind Mice" over the public address system as the umpires made their way to home plate. I doubt if they could get away with that any more because I recently heard that an umpire ejected the PA guy along with the team's manager because he played pre-recorded "boos" over the loud speaker as an argument over a disputed call, that took place on the field.

Umpires are probably the most abused participants in any game. They are always going to be half-right and half-wrong, no matter how they call it. One team will like the decision and the other won't. Umpires try to be impartial and call them like they see them, despite what Ogden Nash once wrote:

> There once was an umpire whose vision
> Was cause for abuse and derision
> He remarked in surprise,
> "Why pick on my eyes?
> It's my heart that dictates my decisions."

Most fans think of umpires as no-nonsense enforcers of the rules. When somebody comes along like a Ron Luciano it is such a refreshing change that the fans, who hardly ever side with umpires, loved Luciano. He tried to entertain the fans as well as make the right calls.

Umpire Ken Kaiser, in his book *Planet of the Umps* said Luciano once came over to him during the game and asked if he could borrow a dollar. Kaiser loaned him a buck and then started wondering. "We're in the middle of a game. What does he need money for?" Between innings he found out. Luciano went straight to the concession stand and bought a hot dog.

No matter how you view umpiring decisions you have to admit the ump is always in control. As umpiring legend Bill Klem told a batter who anticipated a pitch being called a ball and started to first base. Come back son, "It ain't nothing 'til I call it."

Just as we have to trust an umpire's judgment, so are we called on to trust our Heavenly Father's judgment as he listens to our prayers. Peter tells us that He judges fairly and impartially. As the *Sports Devotional Bible* says, "God is absolutely just and He considers each person's situation fairly. This is one of the reasons we can trust Him. He judges from a heart that has compassion for us, yet He does so from a perspective that demands justice. And because of who He is, He is perfect in all His judgments.

While earthly (umpires) strive for correct rulings, God judges rightly in every situation, for He cannot err. Therefore, it is up to us to live "in reverent fear" realizing how vital it is that we maintain an unwavering faith in God. He rules and reigns with both His eyes and His heart, and He rules correctly 100% of the time."

God is the umpire of life. He's in control of the game. No sense arguing that point. Think about how many times a player or a manager wins an argument with an umpire. With God we don't have to worry that He'll make the wrong call.

Big Inning Baseball Quote #41:

The ump is in control according to a manager who learned the hard way:

"You argue with the umpire because there is nothing else you can do about it."

--Leo Durocher--

Diamond Lesson #42

The Hotfoot

Don't let anyone under pressure to give in to evil say, "God is trying to trip me up." God is impervious to evil and puts evil in no one's way. **James 1:16 (The Message)**

Leave it to a rookie to be caught up in the magic of the moment. Florida State University freshman outfielder Derrick Smith had just hit his first collegiate home run on March 14, 2003. He was pumped when he came back to the dugout and his teammates knew it. Smith was ripe for the picking. He was setup for one of baseball's oldest practical jokes.

When Smith hit the top of the dugout steps after taking a "curtain call" at the request of the Seminole fans, he was all smiles. Senior Chris Hart came over to him and feigned great interest in just how the youngster was able to hit it out of the park. He asked about the kind of pitch Smith hit and at what point did he know it was going out, and a lot of other small talk.

While this was happening senior first baseman Jerrod Brown sneaked up behind Smith and put a piece of tape on the heel of his shoe. Attached to the tape was a long piece of paper, which Brown proceeded to light with a match. The attention of the whole dugout was riveted on that flaming piece of paper headed towards Smith's shoe while the Vienna, (pronounced vy-in-uh) Georgia-flash was explaining his hitting heroics.

Suddenly, Smith felt some real heat on his foot, looked back, saw the fire and started dancing wildly to put out the fire. The whole dugout was in hysterics. Smith had become a victim of baseballs' oldest practical joke—the hotfoot.

It was fitting that Smith was on the other end of a joke. He was the entertainer in the Seminole clubhouse with his "Vienna" stories. They had to do with how poor everybody was in the small South Georgia town. He said, "My family was so poor that we couldn't afford a mailbox. When we wanted to mail a letter I had to paint my arm red and stand out front with it raised up, so the mail carrier would see it and come on up to the house to pick up the letter." Such is the humor that abounds in baseball. It also tags you as the perfect victim for the hotfoot.

Whenever things are not going well for us and life has given us a hotfoot, there might be a tendency to feel that God has let us down. James, the half-brother of Jesus, says whenever things get hot we should be glad. He says this is an opportunity for learning. Frequently, we learn more when we fail than when we succeed.

The seeds of success are sown in the fertile soil of failure. James doesn't say "if" trouble comes our way, he says "when" trouble comes that we can profit from it. We learn perseverance during these times. That, in turn, develops depth of character. This kind of pressure makes us more mature. God sometimes has to use adversity. It's easy to be kind and gracious when everything is going well. But, how do we act in tough times? It is when life gives us a hotfoot that we really learn to re-adjust our attitude and to go to God for guidance. As James says, God doesn't create evil circumstances to trip us up. God hates evil more than we do. He wants to help us when we fall victims to it. It is as James says, "If you need wisdom—if you want to know what God wants you to do—ask Him and He will gladly tell you." A hotfoot teaches us humility, even in a time of great triumph. The key is that it teaches us, and we learn what we should be thankful for.

Big Inning Baseball Quote #42:

Here's a practical joker talking about the tools of the trade:

"He handed me a tube of Vaseline. I thanked him and gave him a sheet of sandpaper."

---Don Sutton---
Hall of Fame Pitcher on his meeting with Gaylord Perry

Diamond Lesson #43

Walk-Off Homer

The seventh time around the priests sounded the long blast on their horns. When the people heard the sound of the horns they shouted as loud as they could. Suddenly, the walls of Jericho collapsed and the Israelites charged straight into the city from every side and captured it.   Joshua 6: 16,20

When a player hits a walk-off home run he is definitely king of the hill—for that game. He's the hero because when your team is batting last and tied or trailing their opponent and a player hits a home run, everyone walks off the field. Game Over! Home team wins because of the blast. It is the ultimate individual accomplishment in a team game.

Consequently, it comes as no great surprise that the major league record for most walk-off home runs in a career was shared by some of baseball's superstars. Babe Ruth, Stan Musial, Mickey Mantle, Jimmie Foxx, and Frank Robinson all had 12 walk-off homers in their illustrious, Hall of Fame careers. Then along came Jim Thome who passed all the greats by hitting 13 walk-off homers.

Perhaps, one of the most memorable walk-off homers in World Series action came off the bat of a player who won't make the Hall of Fame. In fact, he wasn't even a starter in many of the games during his seven seasons with the New York Giants. His manager, Leo Durocher, once explained why Dusty Rhodes spent a lot of time on the bench. "Any time you see a fielder get under a ball and pound his glove-even in Little League-you know he's going to catch it. I've seen Rhodes pound his glove and have the ball fall 20 feet behind him."

145

But, on September 29, 1954, in Game One of the World Series at the Polo Grounds nobody was thinking about Dusty's fielding ability. The Giants were playing a heavily favored Cleveland Indian team that had won a record 111 games. Bob Lemon and Sal Maglie locked up in a brilliant pitchers duel that went into the 10th inning tied 2-2. With two men on base, Durocher called on Rhodes to hit.

When Rhodes hit a long fly ball that settled in the right field stands nobody cared about his fielding inadequacies. Dusty had won game one for the Giants with a walk off homer that set the stage for a surprising four game sweep for the New Yorkers.

Following God's instructions Joshua led the Israelites to an Old Testament equivalent of a walk off homer in unusual fashion. After forty years of wilderness wandering the Israelites had crossed the Jordan River and were ready to take the Promised Land. One major roadblock stood in the way—the city of Jericho.

One of the oldest cities in the world, Jericho had walls that were 25 feet high and 20 feet thick. To the outside world Jericho presented the picture of an impenetrable fortress. Instead of getting discouraged Joshua sought God's direction.

He was told to have his entire army march around the city walls once a day for six days. Joshua could have wondered what kind of a plan that was. Sounded like a waste of time to wait almost a week, when the Israelites were ready to attack, but Joshua did as he was instructed.

On the seventh day, per instructions, they marched around the city seven times with the priests blowing horns. On the seventh time the priests gave a loud blast, the people shouted, and the walls of Jericho collapsed. Patience and obedience had paid off as the Israelites won the big one with a walk off homer from the Lord.

Big Inning Baseball Quote #43:

If it took a walk off homer to win the game, this guy could do it:

"You used to think if the score was 5-0, he would hit a five run homer."

---Reggie Jackson---
about Willie Mays

Diamond Lesson #44

Framing the Pitch

Jacob replied, "It's Esau, your older son. I've done as you told me. Here is the wild game cooked the way you like it. Sit up and eat it so you can give me your blessing.
Genesis 27:19

The art of illusion. The primary tool of a magician. Sometimes a catcher has to perform like a magician behind home plate. The best catchers are not really trying to fool the umpire as much as they are trying to create an illusion that a pitch is a strike. Maybe the pitch was slightly outside or just off the inside corner of the plate. If a catcher can frame the pitch so it looks good to the umpire, he could add inches to the strike zone for an entire game.

The most artful catcher will catch the ball out in front of his body so the umpire gets a good look at it. His body will slightly sway as he catches the ball and the glove will turn back in towards the plate giving the illusion that where the glove ends up is where the ball crossed the plate. In reality, the pitch may have been outside or inside but the body swaying and glove turning makes it look like a strike.

All the catcher's movements have to be smoothly orchestrated. If he jerks his glove back towards the plate the ump will automatically call the pitch a ball. Moving the arm towards the center of the plate after receiving a pitch could result in a ball being called. It's important to smoothly, almost imperceptively, twist the glove while trying to hold the arm straight. Then the catcher must leave it framed for a second until he gets the call he wants. "Strike Three!"

Some people would say that a good catcher is stealing strikes, San Francisco's Buster Posey disagrees. On MLB.com Buster explained: "It's more about catching the tough strikes and making them look like strikes and keeping them as strikes."

Talk about a master illusionist! That was Jacob. By creating an illusion, he changed history. The custom was for the father to pronounce his blessing on the eldest son putting him in charge of all his wealth. Esau was eldest; Jacob was second in line.

When Isaac was very old and nearly blind he decided it was time to bless his eldest son Esau who was a great hunter. He requested that Esau go out and kill some wild game and prepare a savory meal for him, then receive his blessing. In those days a person's word was as binding as a written contract. Esau knew once he received his father's blessing he would be in the money.

Meanwhile, Jacob's mother overheard the conversation and plotted to deceive Isaac into blessing Jacob, her favorite son, instead. She prepared the meal of wild game and told Jacob to take it in to Isaac and receive the blessing intended for Esau.

Jacob questioned this because Esau was a hairy, rugged hunter who always smelled of the outdoors. So, Rebekah made him a pair of hairy gloves from goat's skin and fastened a strip of goat's skin around his neck. Then, she instructed Jacob to take the meal to his father and receive the blessing.

Isaac called him to come close and as he felt his hands said. "The voice is Jacob's, but the hands are Esau's. Is it really you Esau?" Jacob lied and continued to play the role of his brother. Isaac ate and then blessed Jacob saying, "May you be the master of your brothers." (Genesis 27:29).

Later Esau came back and presented a meal to Isaac. Then Isaac began to tremble as he related that he had already given the blessing away. Esau cried out, "Bless me too Father." Alas, Isaac replied, "It is too late. Your brother has received your blessing." Esau realized his brother Jacob had framed him by creating an illusion.

Big Inning Baseball Quote #44:

Obviously this pitcher got his share of "framed" third strikes.

"He went out and painted the town beige."

---Vin Scully---
Dodger announcer on quiet Burt Hooton's celebration
of the 1981 World Series

Diamond Lesson #45

Triple

Peter declared, "Even if everyone else deserts you, I never will." Jesus replied, "Peter, the truth is, this very night before the rooster crows, you will deny me three times.
Matthew 26:33-34

If you take a look at the baseball record books and search for triples you'll find that hitting the ball and getting all the way to third base has become a rarity. The Baseball Almanac shows that there is no active player in the Major Leagues among the 100 top triple-hitters of all time.

Sam Crawford who broke in with Cincinnati in 1899, but played most of his career in Detroit with Ty Cobb, is the major league record holder with 309 triples. Crawford retired from baseball in 1917. He passed away in 1968. Cobb, who retired in '29, is second in career triples with 295, while Honus Wagner (1897-1917) who played mostly with Pittsburgh, has the NL record with 252.

Normally, to hit a triple requires a combination of power and speed. Sometimes a crazy bounce in the outfield, or a fielder falling down or some unusual occurrence results in the batter getting a triple. Today's outfields are generally smaller than they were in the early days of baseball, so fielders usually flag down a ball before a triple results. In 1901, 1,238 triples were hit by the 16 teams in the major leagues. In contrast, the 29 big league teams playing in 2013 managed 466 fewer triples. Whenever a modern day batter hits a triple it becomes one of the most exciting occurrences in baseball.

There is a memorable triple mentioned in the Bible. It concerns the three times Peter denied that he knew Jesus. Even though it had been forecast and Peter had strongly denounced this premonition it happened any way.

Fear is such a powerful emotion that it can defeat even the best of intentions. Peter took pride in being a strong defender of Jesus. He was the disciple who was quick to react, even cutting off the ear of the high priest's servant when they came to take Jesus to trial. He was adamant that he would fight to the finish to defend his Lord.

But on the eve of his arrest Jesus tried to explain what was going to happen. It was going to be bad. He knew this. He really didn't blame his disciples for being afraid. He told them, "Tonight all of you will desert me. For the scriptures say, 'God will strike the Shepherd and the sheep of His flock will be scattered.' "

Peter said "Even if everyone deserts you, I never will." To this Jesus replied, "Peter the truth is this very night before the rooster crows you will deny me three times."

Peter had the best of intentions until the populace became unruly and Jesus was arrested. He was sitting in the courtyard when a servant girl came over and said, "You were one of those with Jesus the Galilean. Peter denied it in front of everyone."

Two more times he was confronted by different people and Peter denied knowing Jesus. Just then the rooster crowed and "Peter went away, crying bitterly."

With that third denial Peter had completed the triple he never wanted to happen.

Big Inning Baseball Quote #45:

One way to stop triples is to have this guy in the outfield:

"Willie Mays and his glove. Where triples go to die."

---Fresco Thompson---
Dodger Executive

Diamond Lesson #46

Cutter

All day long you plot destruction. Your tongue cuts like a sharp razor; you're an expert at telling lies.   Psalm 52:2

Since 1996 opponents of the New York Yankees knew that they needed to be ahead of the pin stripers going into the ninth inning or they were history. Sometimes even the eighth inning was too late if they trailed by a run or more. The reason: Mariano Rivera. No matter if you like or dislike the Bronx Bombers, it would be hard not to admire the work of Rivera.

Through the end of the 2013 regular season when the Panama native retired, Rivera had collected 652 saves to go with 82 wins as the Yankees closer. He did that by mixing a four-seam fastball with his best pitch, a cut fastball, also called a cutter.

A batter has only a milli-second to recognize what pitch is on its way to the plate, get the bat started and swing in the proper area to maximize contact. With Rivera pitching the hitter might think he is getting the four-seam fastball when his swing begins only to discover he has been duped and is getting the 95 mph cutter.

The cut fastball, which requires slightly more pressure from the tip of the middle finger on the seam, has a devastating effect on the hitter. For example, Rivera's cutter moves away from right hand batters and in on the fists of left handers. In fact, this pitch can be so destructive to a left hand hitter's at-bat that he may lose his favorite bat. On July 16, 2005, Rivera broke two of the Redsox Johnny Damon's bats during one at-bat. That was not a record for Rivera, however. In the 1999 World Series, pitching against the Atlanta Braves, Rivera broke three of Ryan Klesko's bats during one memorable at-bat. (http.wikipedia.org)

The cutting effect of a pitcher's cut-fastball causes frustration and defeat for hitters. There is an instrument that is even more devastating, although it is smaller than a baseball. It's the tongue! According to the Bible the tongue can be sharper than a two-edged sword.

Someone who is skilled at lying is offensive to God. In Psalm 52 David points out that it is easy to mistake an accomplishment for goodness. (NLT) When David was running from King Saul who was out to kill him, he presented himself to the priest Ahimelech. They didn't realize that Doeg the Edomite saw them when he came there for purification rites.

Doeg reported back to Saul, not only where David was, but also lied and said that the priest was conspiring with Acavic against the king. Saul, being a very insecure and jealous king, told Doeg to kill all the priests. "Doeg turned on them and killed them, eighty-five priests in all, all still wearing their priestly tunics."

This is what David was talking about when he said that Doeg was boasting about his evil deed and building it up as something to be applauded. David told Doeg (Ps 52:5-6). "But God will strike you down once and for all. He will pull you from your home and drag you from the land of the living. The righteous will see it and be amazed. They will laugh and say. Look what happens to mighty warriors who do not trust God."

A cutting remark like a cut fast ball can make a lasting impact.

Big Inning Baseball Quote #46:

Hitting a cut fastball requires strict concentration says this outfielder:

"It's hard for me to concentrate on hitting against Curt Schilling if I'm thinking

about G-Minor."

---Bernie Williams---
Yankees, on why he doesn't play guitar during the season

Diamond Lesson #47

Pitching Rotation

Come to me, all you who are weary and burdened and I will give you rest.
Matthew 11:28

Four man or five man rotation? That's the question. Will a team's pitching staff be more effective if the starters get that extra day of rest or do they need to start every fourth day to stay sharp? Earl Weaver had the answer. "It's easier to find four starting pitchers than it is five," said the Orioles manager in his 1984 book *Weaver on Strategy.*

Obviously if a team had a four-man rotation in which each starter was able to make every scheduled start that would cover 160 of the 162 scheduled games. That never happens for a variety of reasons such as injuries, illness, and ineffectiveness.

Up until the 1970's most teams went with a four man rotation. Then in the early 70's the Dodgers experimented with a five man rotation that included Claude Osteen, Don Sutton, Bill Singer, Al Downing, and Tommy John. Soon everybody but Weaver's Orioles featured five man rotations. With Jim Palmer, Dave McNally, and Mike Cuellar heading the staff and throwing in Tom Phoebus or Jim Hardin for that fourth spot, Baltimore ran away with the pennants in 1969 and 1970, so Weaver saw no reason to change.

Back in the days of the Gashouse Gang, St. Louis Cardinals' starting pitcher Dizzy Dean had the solution for the pitching rotation dilemma. He figured all the Cards needed was a two-man rotation that included himself and his brother Paul. Before the 1934 season began Dizzy boldly proclaimed that he and Paul would win 45 games. He was wrong! They won 49— Dizzy, 30, and Paul, 19.

Once when the Dean brothers pitched both ends of a doubleheader against the Dodgers, Dizzy started it off by pitching a three-hit shutout. When Paul followed up with a no-hitter, Dizzy was hurt. He went over to his brother and said, "Why didn't you tell ole Diz you was going to pitch a no-hitter? If I'd a knowed that I would have pitched one, too."

Obviously a team's starting rotation depends on how many good pitchers they have and some pitchers need more rest than others. Similarly we need more rest some times than others. It isn't always a physical need either. Sometimes we just need a mental break. We need to get away, change environments, and escape the stress.

Jesus was describing this kind of a situation in Matthew 11. He knew that troubles and frustrations could build up to the point where a person felt he just couldn't go on. Sometimes problems beat us down. We feel defeated and we can't find the keys to victory. We just can't seem to get back on track.

Jesus says that He has the solution. Just lay those burdens at His feet. He will gladly show you a solution. He will give you rest. "The rest that Jesus promises is love, healing and peace with God, not the end of all labor." (NLT) He relieves your mind and frees you from the heavy burdens. "A relationship with God changes meaningless, wearisome toil into spiritual productivity."

Just by taking the problem to Jesus we feel better about it already. Then, this freedom clears the way for us to succeed and to become a productive member of the rotation.

Big Inning Baseball Quote #47:

Obviously this pitcher would have been better off with a one man rotation:

"I never slept when I lost. I'd see the sun come up without ever having closed my eyes.

I'd see those base hits over and over and they would drive me crazy."

--Robin Roberts—
Phillies, Hall of Fame Starter

Diamond Lesson #48

On Deck

The cries of the people of Israel have reached me and I have seen how the Egyptians have oppressed them with heavy tasks. Now go, for I am sending you to Pharaoh. You will lead my people, the Israelites out of Egypt. Exodus 3:9-10

"Save me my ups." It's a request you often hear echoing across the sandlots of baseball. Taking practice swings in the on-deck circle, a would-be batter shouts this to the one batting with two-outs. In other words, don't make the last out or I won't get to bat.

When the final out is made nobody really remembers who was in the on deck circle helplessly waiting to hit. Seldom is it even recalled who made the last out in the game. Most of the focus is on who won, who lost and who performed well. Looking good or wearing a menacing scowl while standing in the on deck circle swinging a bat with a weighted donut on it has little post game value.

I wonder how many bad pitches have been made and how many games have been won or lost not because of who is batting, but who is in the on-deck circle? Pitchers are certainly aware of who the most dangerous hitters in the lineup are. They also know which hitters they personally have more success with and the ones they don't fare so well against.

Sometimes pitchers are so concerned with having to face a Hank Aaron or a Ted Williams, who is in the on-deck circle that they make a mistake with the current batter who hurts them with a run-scoring hit on a pitch that is too good. By trying to keep from walking the batter they throw him a fat pitch. Or perhaps by focusing less on the batter and more on who is coming up next, they inadvertently walk the batter and have to face the more dangerous hitter anyway. There's no doubt about it. The on-deck circle plays a role in a baseball game no matter if the player standing in it actually gets to bat or not.

The on-deck batter has to be ready when he is called on to bat. Moses was in God's on-deck circle, but he wasn't ready. He had escaped from Egypt after killing an Egyptian who was abusing a Hebrew slave. He was now happily married to the daughter of a Midianite priest. Life was tranquil and good for Moses.

Moses had been chosen, from the minute he was born, to rescue his people from slavery. That had not changed. God told Moses to go back to Egypt and help his people escape.

Moses protested. He said that the Israelites would not believe that he was to be the rescuer. As miserable as their lives were they had gotten used to being slaves. God gave Moses a few signs to use to make them believers. Little things…like throwing his rod to the ground and having it turn into a serpent; putting his hand inside his cloak where it turned leprous, then healing it when it was put inside again; and pouring water from the River Jordan on the ground where it turned to blood.

All these things got the people's attention. Hopefully God doesn't have to do anything as dramatic as the magic feats he entrusted Moses with to get our attention. God is calling us daily to grow His kingdom. We may simply be in the on-deck circle in some of His plans but our time will come. We want to be ready when it is time to step up to the plate.

Big Inning Baseball Quote #48

Sometimes it is a little confusing in the on deck circle.

"Jesus Alou is in the on-deck circus."

-Jerry Coleman-
Padres announcer

Diamond Lesson #49

Head First Slide

Oh that you would bless me and extend my land.   1 Chronicles 4:10

When going full speed into a base there are three things a runner can do. Obviously, if there is no throw and the runner will be safe, he goes in standing up. On a close play he must decide whether to slide feet first or head first.

Those who slide headfirst feel it is a quicker way to get to the base. With your arms extended you sometimes have the opportunity to reach around the fielder and avoid the tag on those bang-bang plays. The disadvantage of this slide is its openness to injury. It's easy to jam a finger into the base or the baseman and break or dislocate it. The head first slider has to be very careful where his hands end up on the play. This is especially true when sliding into home where the catcher's shin guards present a real hazard. When executed properly the head first slide can be very effective in scoring a run or advancing an extra base.

The alternative, the feet first slide, is sometimes call the "bent-leg" slide because one leg remains straight and goes past the base, while the bent leg may hit the corner of the base or hit it more solidly in the middle. With the advent of breakaway bases that have more give to them than the old stationary bases fewer injuries occur from this slide when properly executed.

One of the more famous headfirst slides in All Star Game history is still surrounded in controversy. Pete Rose scored from second base with the National Leagues's game winning run in the 1970 season, but not without some rough stuff.

Rose, who was solidly built, bowled over AL catcher Ray Fosse, who couldn't hold onto the ball because of the force of the blow delivered by Rose. The Reds All Star player said he was going into his head first slide, but when he saw Fosse's position he changed his mind. By slamming into Fosse, Rose won the game for the NL, but also rearranged Fosse's shoulder to the extent that it still aches from arthritis that has set in.

Maybe that famous head first slide that really wasn't one could have been most accurately described in Padres radio announcer Jerry Coleman's words. He once described a player, "sliding into second with a standup double."

A slide enlarges a player or team's territory. In 1 Chronicles we have the description of an Old Testament person who was able to enlarge his territory by praying for it.

The Prayer of Jabez received lots of attention in the late 1990's into 2000. Bruce Wilkinson's book attracted a lot of attention to a couple of verses of scripture that hadn't previously received a lot of attention. This scripture appears right in the middle of a long list of Who was Who's son, a long chronological family listing.

In 1 Chronicles 4, after listing the sons of Ashur, Naarah, Helah and Hakoz the writer stops and says in verses 9-10, "And Jabez was more honorable than his brethren…Jabez called on the God of Israel saying, Oh, that you would bless me indeed and enlarge my territory. Let your hand be with me, and keep me from harm so that *I will* be free from pain. "

Jabez slid head first into a big request of God and it worked out well. The final words of the scripture before resuming the tedious list of sons, said simply, "And God granted his request. "

Big Inning Baseball Quote #49:

This guy would do anything to win, even if it required a head first slide into home:

"Without him the Cubs would finish in Alberquerque."

---Jimmy Dykes---
Manager, on Ernie Banks

Diamond Lesson #50

Seventh Inning Stretch

By the seventh day God had finished the work He had been doing; so on the seventh day He rested from all His work.   Genesis 2:2

It's a tradition! In ballparks all over America when the bottom of the seventh inning rolls around all the fans stand up. It's called the seventh-inning stretch. A way of getting those muscles loosened up after seven innings of sitting. So, how did all this get started? Nobody knows for sure, but there are a lot of rumors.

According to A. J. Jacobs, author of *Know it all,* one of the more interesting stories credits William Howard Taft, the 27th president of the United States with starting the tradition. Taft was attending a game in Washington where he had presumably eaten quite a few peanuts, Cracker Jacks, etc. In the seventh inning the President, feeling slightly cramped with his 300 pound frame scrunched into the wooden seat decided to stand up and stretch. The crowd, upon seeing the President stand, thought he was getting ready to leave and also stood in respect. When he didn't leave they remained standing, thus the seventh-inning stretch was born.

Taft's story is a nice colorful little tale that gives a good explanation, however it might not be the proper one. The first reference to the seventh-inning stretch actually occurred when Cincinnati Red Stockings player Harry Wright talked about the ritual at the games in which the "spectators all arise between halves of the seventh inning, extend their legs and arms and sometimes walk out."

Other historians say that in 1882, Brother Jasper, who was the first base coach of the Manhattan College baseball team, saw fans getting a little antsy as the games wore on. He mandated a seventh-inning "unwinding of the limbs" at baseball games that worked well and continued on. No matter how it began, the seventh-inning stretch is a nice restful diversion from the stress of pulling for your team to win the game.

Maybe the seventh inning stretch goes all the way back to the beginning of creation. God was busy working on creating the world for six days. He made the heavens and the earth, the waters, dry ground, night and day, animals and man. That's a lot of work in six days. It was time for a rest.

"By the seventh day God had finished the work He had been doing so on the seventh day He rested from all his work. And God blessed the seventh day and made it holy, because on it He rested from all the work of creating that He had done."

So there you have it: The real seventh inning stretch was when God set the example. His message to us is to work hard, but take time to rest. Worship Him and give thanks, then enjoy the fruits of your labor.

Big Inning Baseball Quote #50:

This guy doesn't need a 7th inning stretch to bring the fans to their feet:

"When I'm on the road my greatest ambition is to get a standing boo."

---Al Hrabosky---
Pitcher called "The Mad Hungarian"

Diamond Lesson #51

Bases on Balls

If you know the right thing to do and don't do it, that for you is evil.   **James 4:17**

"Oh those bases on balls!" Dizzy Dean used to quote his manager Frankie Frisch whenever a pitcher's free pass count was mounting up on a televised game he was broadcasting. It's a familiar lament in baseball—one that puts gray hairs on a pitching coach's head.

The base on balls or walk as it is commonly referred to can take the bat out of a dangerous hitter's hands or get a pitcher in deep trouble. Still, walks can be overcome. Hall of Famer Nolan Ryan walked 2,795 batters in his career. He offset those numbers by striking out 5,714 batters. Slugger Reggie Jackson said, "Nolan Ryan's the only guy who puts fear in me. Not because he could get me out, but because he could kill me. You just hoped to mix in a walk so you could have a good night and go 0 for 3."

On the other side of the ledger Babe Ruth struck out 1,330 times but offset that by far with 2062 walks and 714 home runs. With Lou Gehrig batting behind the Babe, those walks frequently turned into runs. The Babe scored 2,174 times.

Walks are frustrating not only for a pitcher or pitching coach, but for the hitter as well. A batter carries a bat to the plate for one reason. He wants to hit the ball. A base on balls doesn't allow him to do that. If he is not patient and swings at bad pitches instead of settling for the walk then his batting average will suffer. The team will be hurt as well as scoring opportunities will turn into outs.

Not walking batters has its own rewards. A fellow by the name of Cy Young holds the AL record for the fewest walks of 250+ innings in a season by issuing only 25 free passes. Maybe that's why he won the most games (511) of anybody to play the game. It could also be the reason the Cy Young Award is given to baseball's best pitcher each year.

Obviously, a pitcher knows he must get the ball over the plate to keep from walking a batter, but he is not always able to do that. Likewise, James says that if we know what is the right thing to do and don't do it that is a sin. In other words, not doing something, if we know what should be done, is as bad as intentionally doing the wrong thing.

The NLT Bible says (pg. 1991) "We tend to think that doing wrong is sin. James tells us that sin is also not doing right. (These kinds of sins are sometimes called sins of commission and sins of omission.) It is a sin to lie; it can also be wrong to know the truth and not tell it." We shouldn't speak evil of someone, but it is also wrong to avoid that person when you know he or she needs your friendship."

The Quest Study Bible (pg. 1681) adds: "When we realize how much good we leave undone, we realize how far we are from God's standards. It is easy to be overcome with guilt. The grace of God can reassure us that there is no condemnation. We fall short, but we fall into the safety net of grace."

The comforting thing is that we may do wrong or we may fail to do good. God will not fail to forgive us if we sincerely and, in a spirit of repentance, seek His forgiveness. When God forgives, the error is wiped out and forgotten.

When a pitcher follows a base on balls with a strikeout, the walk is forgiven.

Big Inning Baseball Quote #51:

Good advice for avoiding those bases on balls:

"When I got to the mound catcher Johnny Oates reminded me that the lower mask was his and the upper one was the umpire's."

> **---Doyle Alexander---**
> **Orioles pitcher**

Diamond Lesson #52

Unis

Now Israel loved Joseph more than any of his other sons, because he had been born to him in his old age; and he made a richly ornamented robe for him. **Genesis 37:3**

In 1882 someone had a bright idea to spruce up the grand old game of baseball by adding color to the uniforms. Back in 1849 the New York Knickerbockers introduced the first baseball unis— white flannel shirts, blue pantaloons, and a straw hat.

Some 33 years later, someone (nobody is taking credit) thought it would be a good idea to colorize the game. It was decided to designate a player's position by the color of his uniform. The first basemen wore red and white striped shirts and caps. The shortstop wore solid maroon, etc. The only way to determine a player's team was all his teammates wore the same color stockings. This fad lasted until mid-season.

In 1888, Washington, Detroit and Brooklyn introduced pinstripes to the world of baseball. Collarless uniform shirts arrived in 1906. Numbered jerseys came to the Majors in 1929 when the Cleveland Indians became the first Major League team to put numbers on the backs of their uniforms. They beat the Yankees in unveiling the new fad by a day because New York's game was rained out.

In 1912 the Yankees adopted the pinstriped uniforms they still wear. The St. Louis Cardinals first wore their current "birds on a bat" in 1922. The Dodgers put their name in script letters in 1938. The Braves placed a tomahawk on their uniforms in 1946.

The uniform has become an important part of the national pastime. "There is something special about the baseball uniform, a mystique that is hard to pin down. Whether we are looking at someone in a uniform or trying it on ourselves it is the feeling of the fabric, the design on the cap and jersey, the colors, cut, and history of the outfit that all lend meaning to our relationship with the game." <u>www.baseballhalloffame.org</u>

Just as the uniform sets players apart, Joseph looked a lot different from his brothers when he donned the fancy new coat his Dad made for him. We read in Genesis that it was a coat of many colors. It was full length and fancy. Joseph was hot stuff when he put it on and he let his brothers know it.

With a brash, teenage cockiness Joseph lorded it over his brothers. Not only wearing his fancy coat, but also bringing up some dreams he had that made him special. In the first dream he told them they were all in the field binding sheaves when all of a sudden his sheaf rose up and the other sheaves bowed down to it. Later, he related a dream in which the sun, moon, and eleven stars were bowing down to him. These dreams were not well received by his brothers. They took off his fancy coat and threw him down a dry well. When a caravan of slave traders came along they sold Joseph to them and he was carted off to Egypt.

This set up the big lie they told their father, Israel, that they found Joseph's coat with blood on it. They speculated that a wild animal had devoured him. Joseph ended up being governor of Egypt and his brothers did indeed bow down to him. His uniform (coat) played a major part in those dreams coming true. Joseph gave hope to all who are mistreated, when he told his brothers "You intended to harm me, but God intended it for good to accomplish what is now being done, the saving of many lives." Joseph's uniform had led to the fulfillment of his dreams. (Genesis 50:20)

Big Inning Baseball Quote #52:

Here's a guy who was proud to put on the uniform.

"Baseball is such a great life that anyone who complains about it, I think is a little clouded. I could never find the time to complain."

---Jim Lonborg---
Redsox Pitcher

Diamond Lesson #53

Opening Day

...to be made new in the attitude of your minds and to put on the new self, created to be like God in true righteousness and holiness.   Ephesians 4:23-24

Opening Day in baseball. There's nothing like it. The die-hard fans have been waiting through the long hard winter for the return of the game. Even those who don't follow the game through the entire season may turn out for the season opener. It's an event. Some folks even think that the Major League opening day should be a holiday.

Spring training has presented just enough baseball to whet the appetites of the fans, but everybody knows those games don't count. A team could win all its spring training games and still be home watching the World Series on TV in October. Everything on opening day counts.

Some of the great names in baseball history have had phenomenal opening days. Frank Robinson specialized in season openers. He is the only player to hit opening day homers for four different teams. He also holds the opening day record for homers with 8 in his career. His last came in 1975 when he was a player/manager having become the first African/American manager in the Big Leagues.

Hall of Fame fire baller Bob Feller took the mound in 35 degree temperatures for Cleveland's opening day game in 1940 despite having pitched an exhibition game two days earlier. Feller walked the bases loaded against the Whitesox in the second inning. The bullpen got active, but he straightened things out and went on to pitch the Majors only opening day no-hitter. Feller would pitch three opening day shutouts in his career.

Getting a win on opening day doesn't guarantee success for the season. The St. Louis Browns won every opening day game from 1937 to 1945, yet notched only one pennant in 52 seasons. Still, their fans felt good on opening day.

When we become believers in Jesus Christ it is like opening day. A new life begins. The old ways are changed and all but forgotten. The old stats are still on the books. Yes, the mistakes we made are still a fact, but, they don't have to haunt us any more. They don't have to affect the way we play the game now because it is a new season.

The NLT Bible (pg. 1878) points out: "Our old way of life before we believed in Christ is completely in the past. We should put it behind us like old clothes to be thrown away. When we decide to accept Christ's gift of salvation, it is both a onetime decision, as well as a daily conscious commitment. We are not driven by desire and impulse. We must put on the new nature, head in the new direction, and have the new way of thinking that the Holy Spirit gives. "

This doesn't mean we won't make mistakes. Unfortunately, we may repeat some of the mistakes we made in the past. As we seek to correct them we know we are forgiven. We are not perfect and never will be. However, the more we trust the Lord the more we can distance ourselves from past mistakes. It is a new day.

Putting our faith and trust in the Lord is the equivalent of a Season Opener in baseball. We have no losses. Our slate is clean. In fact, each day is a brand new day given to us by God that can serve as a season opener for a pennant-winning season in life.

Big Inning Baseball Quote #53

Even the all time greats couldn't wait for baseball season to roll around:

"You look forward to it like a birthday party when you are a kid. You think something wonderful is going to happen."

--Joe DiMaggio--

Diamond Lesson #54

Play By Play

Then Jesus came to them and said, "All authority in heaven and on earth has been given to me. Therefore go and make disciples of all nations, baptizing them in the name of the Father and of the Son and of the Holy Spirit. Matthew 28:19-20

During 23 years of doing play-by-play and color on the Florida State University Baseball radio broadcasts I came to appreciate the importance of accuracy. On occasion, in talking with people about a game they didn't attend and wasn't being televised, they have described a game situation exactly the way my long time partner, the late Lee Bowen, or I described it. They would fiercely defend that viewpoint if anyone said it happened otherwise.

Baseball play-by-play is an art in itself. Fans come to identify with the announcers as much as they do the players. Red Barber, Mel Allen, Russ Hodges, Harry Caray and others have become legends almost as much as Babe Ruth or Hank Aaron or Willie Mays. Their descriptions of historic happenings are as memorable as the events. Remember, "The Giants win the Pennant!" Russ Hodges kept yelling that into the microphone as Bobby Thompson circled the bases to beat the Dodgers. That historic homer completed their miracle run from 13 and one-half games out, to win it all.

Remember Harry Caray always leading the singing of "Take Me out to the Ballgame" during the seventh inning stretch at Cubs games. When he passed away the tradition continued with different celebrities, some who couldn't sing a lick, leading the singing over the PA system. Mike Stoker commemorated Caray's importance to the game, as well as all play-by-play guys, in the following poem after Caray passed away:

> "Where Lou still starts
> And Babe still swings
> Where Johnny still sees
> and Leo still screams
> Where Don still throws
> and Mickey still hits
> Harry still sings."

The play-by-play guys live on in memories just like the players.

In Matthew 28, Jesus tells the disciples to become play-by-play guys. They are to go everywhere and explain the game to everyone. It was His reason for coming to earth and He wanted everyone to know that no matter how dark or depressing the landscape seemed there was hope. They would be able to rally and win the game. Because of Him they would receive salvation.

Verses 19 and 20 are called the Great Commission. Its message is the same today as it was when the disciples first heard it. These are Jesus' last words of instruction to the men he had grown close to. He had fished with them. Worked miracles in their presence. He'd dined with them. Washed their feet. These play-by-play guys were charged with keeping his memory alive, building the church, and dispensing hope.

Jesus told them to make more disciples. He tells us to do the same. We are to spread the word of the salvation that is provided through his life, death, and resurrection. As the NLT Bible (pg. 1474) says: "We are to go---whether it is next door or to another country---and make disciples. It is not an option, but a command to all who call Jesus 'Lord.' We are not all evangelists in the formal sense, but we have all received gifts that we can use to help fulfill the great commission. As we obey, we have comfort in the knowledge that Jesus is always with us." We are his play-by-play people who announce the way things are to others.

Big Inning Baseball Quote #54:

Maybe that's why they called him "Red", because he was always colorful:

"He was running like a bunny with his tail on fire."

Expression of Hall of Fame Broadcaster
---Red Barber---
describing a baseruner

Diamond Lesson #55

3rd Base Coach's Box

For God did not give us a spirit of timidity, but a spirit of power, of love, and of self-discipline.   2 Timothy 1:7

The view is different from the third base coach's box. In 17 years of coaching there the Colonel has seen it all. Chip Baker, FSU's Director of Baseball Operations, has some tall tales to tell from his coaching days that include directing traffic at third base.

Mostly what people remember about a third base coach is when he makes a mistake. If he sends a runner who slides safely in at home the runner is usually credited with good base running. If he waves a runner around third on a ball hit to the outfield and he is thrown out at the plate the coach gets the blame for sending him.

The Colonel went one better. He once had two runners thrown out at the plate on the same play. "We were playing Grambling. Ed Fulton (slow runner) was on second and Steve Taddeo (a little faster) was on first. Luis Alicea hit one off the right field screen. I waved Fulton and Taddeo was on his heels, so they both rounded third, headed for home and the catcher tagged both players out. Umpire Bruce Ravan told me that's the first time he ever motioned a runner out with his left hand. Fulton was ruled out with his right hand and in the bang-bang play, Taddeo was ruled out with Ravan's left."

Of course Baker made enough good decisions to more than offset his mistakes. For example the one that ended the 17-inning game against Miami that was the longest in FSU history. The Seminoles had come from nine runs down to send the game into extra innings. Then, in the 17th with Mike Futrell on first, the Colonel made up his mind if he

183

got a chance to send a runner he would. He waved Futrell around on a ball hit to the outfield and he slid in with the winning run ending the marathon contest.

Baker says that doing your homework is the key to being a good third base coach. Knowing who has a great arm in the outfield, who has one you can challenge and which fielders have weak arms helps make a decision that has to be made in three seconds. Over the years the Colonel made lots of good three-second-decisions to send FSU to the College World Series.

Just as coaching boldness can win ball games, so are we instructed to proceed without timidity in our lives. Timothy was a young preacher who had been Paul's partner on some missionary journeys. While Paul was in prison he was charged with carrying on the work of discipleship.

Apparently Timothy was timid. He was not the most outspoken of people, a marked difference from Paul's personality and approach. When he began to experience opposition to his message it would have been easy for him to falter. Paul urged him to be bold and not be intimidated.

If we allow ourselves to be bullied about by others we can't do our work effectively. Paul reminded Timothy that an effective Christian leader possesses three characteristics: power, love, and self-discipline. These are available because the Holy Spirit lives in us. (NLT, pg. 1939).

Paul pointed out that the power of the Holy Spirit can help us overcome any fear of rejection we might have. Because of this we can boldly proclaim the things we know to be good and right. Like a good third base coach who has done his homework, we can make instant decisions without fear of failure.

Big Inning Baseball Quote #55:

You wouldn't want to be in the coaches' box in this town:

"Philly fans are so mean that on Easter Sunday, when the players staged an Easter-egg hunt for their kids, the fans booed the kids who didn't find any eggs."

---Bob Uecker---

Diamond Lesson #56

Batting Cages, Pitching Machines, Etc.

I will instruct you and teach you in the way you should go. I will counsel you and watch over you.   Psalm 32:8

Most fans never see the batting cage at the baseball stadium. You have to arrive at the park at least two hours before the game to see batting practice. Serious fans get there early just to watch their favorite players bash fastballs into the seats. It's a good warm-up for the game but doesn't usually mean much in determining how a player will perform in the game. Some great outings in the batting cage have been followed by awful game performances. Likewise there have been times when a player is not even hitting the straight-arrow batting practice pitches. He is popping them up, hitting the top of the cage; grounding them in the dirt. Even occasionally whiffing one. Then, he goes out and has a killer game, just crushing normal pitching at every opportunity.

Batting cages are just one of the many pieces of equipment that help players prepare for the games. There are also completely enclosed inside cages where players can get additional swings. They don't even need a pitcher because there are pitching machines to do that. The machines can be set to varying speeds, angles, etc. to enable the player to work on his swing.

And of course videotape machines are everywhere. Anything a player does can be video taped and replayed endlessly to determine where a swing has gotten off track. Players who are slumping can go back and look at video of their swings when they were on a hitting streak and make comparisons. Some players even duck into the clubhouse during a game and look at video of their previous at bat to see what kind of pitches they were getting, what they hit and what they missed. The world of technology, far beyond the first simple batting cages, has now permeated the world of baseball.

Time spent in the batting cage can be considered a time of instruction. Much of it is self-instruction in which the batter works on things he deems to be weaknesses or areas requiring attention. In a way much of our lives are spent in batting cages working to get better in the areas where we sometimes fail.

In many of his Psalms David lamented his shortcomings and asked for God's help. Wisely, he spent much of his time praising God's awesome power to control and change the things that needed correction. The *Believer's Bible Commentary* says it is uncertain if the words in Psalm 32:8-9 are David's or God's. Nevertheless, they make a point well taken. "I will instruct you and teach you in the way you should go." If we are to make the best moves, take the right swings, and go the right way we need to first call on the Lord for His instruction.

In Psalm 33:13 we read, "From the heaven the Lord looks down and sees all mankind. From His dwelling place He watches all who live on earth." God sees everything that everybody does. He has that videotape running 24-7. When we call on Him he will show us the way to go. When we dash out on our own and make the big mistakes He has the video replays to instruct us.

We're cautioned in Psalm 32:9 to not be "like the horse or mule which have no understanding." They have to be controlled by the bit and bridle. We don't. God has given us a brain and a free will. If we practice, daily, seeking his instructions our batting averages will increase as the base hits in life multiply.

Big Inning Baseball Quote #56:

Timing starts in the batting cage:

"Hitting is timing. Pitching is upsetting timing."

---Warren Spahn---

Diamond Lesson #57

The Grounds Crew

Just as our bodies have many parts and each part has a special function, so it is with Christ's body. We are all parts of His one body and each of us has different work to do.   Romans 12:4-5

It's a different kind of pressure. Every bunt or batted ball can have him on the edge of his seat. He's the field supervisor or head groundskeeper on the grounds crew. His job is to make sure the playing field is in "beyond perfect" playing condition. Justin Wilmot, former field supervisor at Dick Howser Stadium in Tallahassee, said he tensed up every time a ground ball was hit in the 2003 Super Regional between Florida State and Notre Dame. His greatest fear was that a game of that importance would be decided by a bad hop.

The grounds crew plays a very important role in a baseball game. Not only must they have the field in tip top condition to play on, they must also be ready to get that field covered with a tarp in minutes if it starts to rain.

Redsox head groundskeeper David Mellor has a grounds crew of 35 to help him keep the field in shape. Considering the fact that Fenway Park is 103 years old (2015), it requires a lot of work to keep it in game condition. There's raking, mowing, sweeping, watering, fertilizing and painting to be done.

On top of that Mellor has become of the best in the game at "lawn art" which is the latest rage in ball field décor. Mellor has developed the art of mowing various patterns to perfection. His patterns have included the Redsox logo, a jack o' lantern, the

American flag, and after Ted Williams passed away Mellor mowed his number "9" into the outfield grass.

Mellor told Boston.com correspondent Dave Ropeik that the "trick to lawn art is using a roller to bend different areas of the grass in different directions, so the pattern shows up because each section reflects light differently." They have to change the pattern every few days because Mellor says, "crushing the grass down in the same pattern all the time would affect how the ball rolls." Then he would be tensing up with every ground ball that was hit and the major league season is too long for that.

The apostle Paul pointed out that as Christians each of us has a job to do. He encourages us to do our job well and not get sidetracked. Just like the groundskeeper we have a special talent. The team wouldn't ask the groundskeeper to play shortstop, but they do ask him to have the infield dirt in good condition to enable the shortstop to field the balls hit his way.

In the Message, Romans 12:5-9 he says, "If you preach, just preach God's message, nothing else; if you help, just help, don't take over; if you teach, stick to your teaching; if you give encouraging guidance, be careful that you don't get bossy; if you're put in charge, don't manipulate; if you are called to give aid to people in distress, keep your eyes open and be quick to respond; if you work with the disadvantaged, don't let yourself get irritated with them or depressed by them. Keep a smile on your face."

God gives us these gifts so we can build up his church. If each person does the thing he or she does best the result is a smooth, efficiently run operation. It starts with making an honest appraisal as to what you can do and working within those parameters.

Healthy self-esteem is important. Self-esteem begins with our relationship with Christ.

Apart from him we can't do anything. Working with the gifts He gives us we can't fail.

Big Inning Baseball Quote #57:

The grounds crew can exterminate one of the following:

"Natural grass is a wonderful thing for little bugs and sinkerball pitchers."

---Dan Quisenberry---
Royals Reliever

Diamond Lesson #58

Spit

Then spitting on the man's eyes, he laid his hands on him and asked, "Can you see anything now?" Then Jesus placed His hands over the man's eyes again. As the man stared intently, his sight was completely restored and he could see everything clearly.
Mark 8: 23, 25

It's the scariest sight in baseball. The pitcher winds up, fires the pitch and it takes off, going straight towards the batters head. When the batter hits the dirt, avoiding the pitch, there is a collective sigh of relief.

There was delayed relief on August 17, 1920 when a pitch thrown by Carl Mays of the Yankees hit Indians shortstop Ray Chapman in the head. A few minutes later Chapman was assisted by two teammates as he walked to the dugout to the applause of the fans. However, he died several hours later.

This incident led to the banning of the "spitball" from baseball. It was Mays main pitch. There were 17 pitchers who were "grandfathered in" and allowed to throw the spitter until retirement because they had built their careers on this pitch. The last one was thrown in 1933.

After that no "foreign substances" were allowed to be applied to a baseball by the pitcher. The problem was that a dampened baseball would take an abnormal sharp break and the batter would be hard pressed to avoid being hit.

Thus, ensued a lot of trickery by pitchers. Some became very adept at hiding substances or objects they could use to doctor up baseballs. Gaylord Perry would put Vaseline on his zipper and secretively apply it to the ball. Preacher Roe was famous for concealing, throwing and controlling a spitball. Ted Radcliffe hid an emery board in his belt buckle.

No matter what lengths a pitcher goes to in order to gain an advantage the great hitters will still be successful. Hall of Famer Stan Musial points out the key: "When a pitcher is throwing a spitball don't worry about it. Just hit the dry side like I do."

Jesus used a spitter for good purposes. It was among his greatest miracles and amazed all those who saw Him perform this feat. The people had heard of the miracles Jesus was performing. When He and His disciples came to Bethsaida they brought a blind man to Him for healing.

When they begged Jesus to touch the man, He spit on the man's eyes and then put His hands on him asking him if he could see anything. The man said, "I see people; they look like trees walking around." Then Jesus put his hands on the man again and he was completely healed and could see everything clearly.

Why did Jesus use spit? The Quest Study Bible (pg. 1394) says, "Certainly Jesus, with His divine powers, did not need to spit in order to heal blindness. Several Roman writers, as well as Jewish rabbis consider saliva to be a valid treatment for blindness. In this case Jesus realized the man's need for increased faith and offered His physical action to raise his expectations. If so, the man's spiritual sight was strengthened as physical sight was imparted to him."

Jesus was able to use spit for a good purpose and all who saw his actions knew they had witnessed a true miracle.

Big Inning Baseball Quote #58:

With his talent this pitcher didn't need to throw a spitter.

"I never threw an illegal pitch. The trouble is once in awhile I toss one that ain't never been seen by this generation."

---Satchel Paige---

Diamond Lesson #59

Dugout

Then Jonah went out to the east side of the city and made a shelter to sit under as he waited to see if anything would happen to the city.   Jonah 4:5

It's called the dugout because it is usually slightly below field level and is where a baseball teams' bench is located. The dugout used to provide some privacy for players away from the prying eyes of angry fans after striking out, making an error, or giving up lots of runs. That was before the advent of television's high-powered zoom lenses. Now, if a player is arguing with his manager or slamming a bat into the water cooler, it can all be seen on television and sometimes on the big scoreboard in the outfield.

The Yankees Billy Martin used to be good for a few lively dugout scenes. Billy had a temper and rarely did he keep it in check. Once he went after Reggie Jackson, his star slugger, and players stepped in front of Billy. The cameras caught him duck walking along the bench to avoid the blockade in a determined effort to catch up with Reggie.

Lou Pinella was always good for a few dugout confrontations, especially with the umpires, when he was with the Yankees, then the Mariners, and finally with the Devil Rays (now the Rays). Lou had been known to toss a few items onto the playing surface in protest of an umpiring decision. Then the umpire would walk to the dugout and toss Lou out of the game. That usually got Pinella out of the dugout as he rushed out to protest the umpire's actions. Lots of things go on in the dugout. Sometimes even meaningful strategy that helps win a game takes place there.

Just as the dugout provides shelter from the weather for players after their work on the field is completed, so God provided relief from the heat of day with a leafy plant

196

for Jonah to sit under. Jonah had completed his work, although grudgingly, of preaching to the Ninevites. Now he sought shelter from the sun to await the outcome. He thought he would be watching the destruction of the city from a safe place.

But, in life things don't always turn out as we think or hope they will. Sometimes we expect a certain turn of events, but we have to wait for them to happen. Often we dread what might happen and our worst fears are realized. This does not mean that God is not in control.

This happened to Jonah. He didn't want to preach to the Ninevites, so he foolishly tried to run from God. In this famous Bible story, God caught up with Jonah, who ended up praying for relief from the belly of a whale that had swallowed him.

After God rescued him, Jonah preached to the Ninevites while secretly hoping that they wouldn't listen: but, they did. They repented and their lives were changed. Instead of seeing Nineveh destroyed from his perch under the plant, Jonah saw that God had spared the city. That didn't set too well with him and further aggravation occurred when a worm ate into the plant killing it and leaving Jonah exposed to the heat of the sun.

The Jews didn't want to share God with the Gentiles. God used this lesson to point out the error in Jonah's thinking. Basically, he told Jonah how wrong and silly it was to be angry about His not sparing the sheltering plant, but not care about the destruction of a city of 120,000 people. God changed Jonah's thinking in his dugout.

Big Inning Baseball Quote #59:

The dugout is a friendly place, but you wouldn't want to spend all your time there:

"I think I hold the record for the most games watched… career!"

---Kurt Bevacqua---
former player and bench pro

Diamond Lesson #60

Batting Helmet

In every battle you will need faith as your shield to stop the fiery arrows aimed at you by Satan. Put on salvation as your helmet…   Ephesians 6:16, 17a

At first any player who wore one was called a "sissy." The tough guys said they looked more like miners helmets than something a baseball player would wear while batting. Yes, the batting helmet that is a standard part of the uniform nowadays, did not receive immediate acceptance.

The first batting helmet was created by longtime Pittsburgh traveling secretary Charlie Muse. Thus, the Pirates became the first team to wear them in 1952. For a while some players chose to wear them, but most didn't. Then, in 1954 the Braves Joe Adcock was wearing a batting helmet when he was beaned so severely by Brooklyn's Clem Labine that he was unconscious for 15 minutes. Later Adcock said that the helmet might have saved him from a very serious injury. The next day every Dodger player wore a batting helmet and other teams followed suit.

1971 was the first year in which batting helmets were mandatory in the Majors although players who had not worn them before and didn't want to wear one were grandfathered in and didn't have to abide by the rule.

Now all players are required to wear helmets even while running the bases although the likelihood of getting hit in the head with a ball while running is less than that of getting beaned while batting. Failure to wear a helmet is cause for ejection.

John Olerud, who has played for the Redsox, Blue Jays, Yankees, Mets, and Mariners, wore a batting helmet in the field as well as at the plate. Olerud started wearing the helmet at all times in college. While playing for Washington State University he had to undergo emergency surgery for a cerebral aneurysm. Olerud went directly from college to the majors and compiled a .295 lifetime batting average while playing 17 seasons. This record of success might have prompted a few more players to wear a batting helmet even in the field like Olerud did.

A helmet is an important part of the armor God provides for each of us. We are involved in a war against evil every day. Spiritual warfare for believers, according to the Quest Study Bible (pg. 1619), is fought in the mind, emotions, and the will. Scriptural truth is our primary line of defense. That's why Paul urges us to be renewed in our minds.

But Paul told the Ephesians to put on the full armor that God had provided for them. To be able to stand our ground we need: the belt of truth buckled around our waist; the breastplate of righteousness; the shoes of peace; the shield of faith to extinguish the flaming arrows of the evil one; the sword of the spirit which is the word of God; and then there's that all important batting helmet. It is called the helmet of salvation. It protects us from the sting of death because salvation provided through Jesus Christ trumps even death.

Paul further instructs Christians to "Pray at all times and on every occasion in the power of the Holy Spirit." By doing all this we will equip ourselves so that any errant fast balls that are thrown or hit by the evil one will be fended off by this armor especially our helmet of salvation.

Big Inning Baseball Quote #60:

You definitely needed a batting helmet when confronting this guy:

"Lots of people look up to Billy Martin. That's because he just knocked them down."

---Jim Bouton---
Yankees Pitcher. Author of "Ball Four."

Diamond Lesson #61

Rubber Game

Consider it pure joy my brothers, whenever you face trials of many kinds, because you know that the testing of your faith develops perseverance. Perseverance must finish it's work so you may be mature and complete, not lacking anything.   James 1:2-3

When a team wins the final game of a series that has been tied it is said to have won the "rubber game." What's up with that? Where did that come from? Well, according to *Yahoo.com* and *The Sporting News* the term comes from the card game of Bridge. In bridge when each side has won one of the first two games the deciding game is called the "rubber game." And a set of three games is called a rubber.

If you check out the *Word Detective* it says: "This tie-breaking sense of "rubber" apparently originated in the English game of "bowls" or lawn bowling." The object in the game of bowls is to get a little white ball as close to another ball at the end of the green expanse (lawn) without touching it. When your ball touches the other that is a fatal error. It is "rubbing" against the other ball. This sporting context for "rubber" first appeared in 1599. In 1744, the card playing crowd for games of whist and bridge used the term "rubber" for the match and "rubber game" for the clincher.

But, why rubber? Why is it called that? It is not related to rubber as we know it, those elastic bands that snap back when you pull them and let them go. The ones that are so handy for holding pencils, packages, etc. together. That kind of rubber was first called India-rubber because it came from the East Indies.

Brewer's Dictionary of Phrase and Fable votes for "bowls" as the originator. The logic? The losing team's hopes in the deciding game of a series would be "rubbed out." Therefore, they would lose the "rubber game."

The seventh game of the World Series is always the "rubber game." The Fall Classic has gone to a "rubber game" 36 times (thru 2014). In 1920 the Cleveland Indians beat the Brooklyn Robins, five games to two. That could never happen today because the first team to win four games is the champion. If one team wins four before the other team wins three then there is no "rubber game."

It takes perseverance to win a "rubber game." It is joyful when you win it. James says we should "consider it pure joy" when we are put through these tense, on-edge tests because this kind of testing develops perseverance. Perseverance is a great quality to possess. Its synonyms include persistence, endurance, patience, stamina, backbone, and courage. Without persistence the hard jobs won't get done.

The QSB Commentary on James (pg. 1677) says: "This doesn't mean we derive pleasure from pain. Instead this describes a unique kind of joy—the deep sense of well-being that comes from knowing that God is in control of everything in our lives. It's an assurance that He is constantly at work, using both pain and pleasure to develop within us character traits of endurance and patience.

Getting through the "rubber game" might be stressful, but winning it with God's help provides the ultimate in pleasure.

Big Inning Baseball Quote #61

Apparently rubber games are secondary to this manager.

"When we win I'm so happy I eat a lot. When we lose, I'm so depressed, I eat a lot.

When we're rained out I'm so disappointed I eat a lot."

--Tommy Lasorda—
Dodger Manager

Diamond Lesson #62

Nicknames

No longer will you be called Abram; your name will be Abraham, for I have made you a father of many nations.   Genesis 17:5

Baseball was created for nicknames. The skills required to play the game just lend themselves perfectly to the development of colorful and imaginative nicknames. According to the dictionary a nickname is "an additional or substitute name given to a person, place, or thing; usually descriptive and given in fun, affection, or derision."

One of the early baseball nicknames was Frank "Home Run" Baker of the Philadelphia Athletics, given to him after he led the league in homers in 1911 with a grand total of 11 four baggers. In his 13-year career he hit 96 homers.

An interesting nickname applied to Luke Appling (Whitesox). They called him "Old Aches and Pains."   As Maury Allen wrote in *Big Time Baseball* "…the real blunder was to ask him (Appling), 'How do you feel?' It would sometimes take him a half an hour before he stopped telling you."

The Tigers' "Wahoo" Sam Crawford was born in Wahoo, Nebraska. Roger Bresnahan, who developed into an excellent catcher under John J. McGraw with the Giants, was called the "Duke of Tralee" because he told people he was born in Tralee Ireland. He was actually from Toledo, Ohio.

Mordecai "Three-Finger" Brown won 239 games pitching with only three fingers on his throwing hand. "Sunny Jim" Bottomley's nickname derived from his positive disposition and also his ability to drive in runs—1,422 in 16 years. Ty Cobb was called the "Georgia Peach", but not for his peachy disposition.

There are nicknames so common that everyone knows them. Dizzy Dean; Babe Ruth; Yogi Berra; Hammerin' Hank Aaron; Joltin' Joe Dimaggio; The Splendid Splinter, Ted Williams; Stan "the Man" Musial; "Say Hey" Willie Mays.

In the Bible there are many examples of people who were re-named. One of the earliest and most notable was Abram. God gave him the name Abraham to seal a covenant between them. In ancient Hebrew culture names were changed when a person's circumstances changed. God changed His name and promised him that he would be the father of many nations. This took place when Abraham was 99 years old.

Another person who was renamed by God was the third link in God's plan to uphold his promise to Abraham. Jacob, his grandson, was renamed Israel and became the father of the twelve tribes of Israel.

In the New Testament we find Simon who became a disciple of Jesus. Impetuous, strong-willed, loyal, Simon Peter was named simply "Peter" by Jesus. "Now, I say that you are Peter, and upon this rock I will build my church, and all the powers of hell will not conquer it." (Matthew 16:18).

Saul of Tarsus, a zealous persecutor of Christians was struck blind on the road to Damascus in a life-changing experience. When his eyesight was restored he was renamed Paul and became a zealous promoter of Christ, preaching, establishing churches on missionary journeys and writing. His work comprises the New Testament books of Romans, 1 & 2 Corinthians, Galatians, Ephesians, Philippians Colossians, 1 & 2 Thessalonians, 1 & 2 Timothy, Philemon, and possibly part of Hebrews.

Big Inning Baseball Quote #62:

Well at least they didn't change his name:

"Being traded is like celebrating your 100th birthday. It might not be the happiest occasion in the world, but consider the alternatives."

---Joe Garagiola---

Diamond Lesson #63

All Star Game

Much is required from those to whom much is given and much more is required from those to whom much more is given.   *Luke 12:48*

The All Star game feats that are most fondly spoken of are usually the big hits like Ted Williams' three run shot off the Cubs' Claude Passeau in the bottom of the ninth in Detroit in the 1941 game—a walkoff homer to win for the American League, 7-5.

When it comes to All Star Game pitching performances one game stands above all others even though it happened in the second showcase game played way back in 1939. Southpaw Carl Hubbell, the man called "The Meal Ticket" of the New York Giants, was scheduled to start for the National League against a loaded American League lineup featuring Babe Ruth and Lou Gehrig in the middle of it.

Before the game as starting catcher Gabby Hartnett (Cubs) looked over the lineup he told Hubbell, don't throw anything for strikes except your screwball. Waste everything else. Hubbell's screwball broke the opposite of a lefthander's curveball. It faded away from righties and moved in on the fists of lefties.

After giving up a single to Charlie Gehringer (Tigers) and walking Henie Manush (Senators), Hubbell appeared to have dug his own grave as the Bambino walked to the plate. Four pitches later, three of them twisting screwballs at the knees, Ruth shook his head in amazement as he was called out on strikes.

Pitching the same way to Gehrig, Hubbell stuck him out on four screwballs, the last a swing and a miss. Now, the 50,000 fans at the Polo Grounds were excited as powerful Jimmie Fox (Redsox) stepped in. They exploded when Hubbell struck him out as well.

In the second inning Hubbell struck out Al Simmons (A's) and Joe Cronin (Senators) for an amazing five consecutive strikeouts of five of baseball's best. That's why Hubbell's feat is still elevated to the top of the best All Star performances.

When Jesus was teaching he said those to whom much was given much would be expected from them in the way of service. Those who were given more would be expected to accomplish even more. *The Message* says: "Great gifts mean great responsibilities; greater gifts mean greater responsibilities."

The *Believer's Bible Commentary* states: "Those who have come to know God's will as it is revealed in the Scriptures are under great responsibility to obey it. Much has been given to them; much will be required of them."

When you see a player who is a member of an All Star team you expect superior performance from him. As a member of His team Jesus expects more than the ordinary from us because He looks on each of us as All Stars. God didn't make any rejects. We will not be held responsible for gifts we do not have. He expects us to use the gifts we have received to do all the good we can do. At times it may seem difficult, but the reward is worth it.

Big Inning Baseball Quote #63:

When these All Stars talk everybody listens:

"They invented the All Star Game for Willie Mays."

---Ted Williams---

Diamond Lesson #64

The Curse

By the sweat of your brow you will eat your food.   *Genesis 3:19*

"A month ago they were calling us chokers. But, now they are calling us something else that starts with a C-H---champions," said Chicago catcher A.J. Pierzynski, in October 2005, after his White Sox had swept the Houston Astros in the World Series to become the champions of baseball.

What the ChiSox had accomplished, even beyond winning a World Series, was to end a so-called curse that dated back about 88 years. 1919 was the darkest year in baseball history. It was the year the White Sox became known as the Black Sox because eight of their players were accused of throwing the World Series against Cincinnati. The disgraced players, including Shoeless Joe Jackson one of baseball's best, were banned from the game of baseball for life.

In 1906 and 1917 the White Sox won the Series but had never won another one since the Black Sox scandal. The 2005 edition featured a different breed of White Sox. These guys could really play the game. Not only did they sweep the World Series but they occupied first place every day of the season. That was a feat accomplished in the American League only by the fabled 1927 New York Yankees.

When told what prestigious company the Sox were now a part of, World Series MVP Paul Konerko responded to Jayson Stark of ESPN.com, "I don't think we are exactly the '27 Yankees. We've got no Babe Ruth. We don't even have a Roger Maris. We do have the Three Stooges, though, me, Joe Crede (3b) and Aaron Rowand (cf): Ro,

Mo, and Yo." Stooges or Superstars? It didn't matter because this unlikely cast of characters, through hard work and a blue collar mentality, ended an 88 year old curse.

There is a curse that mankind was put under that goes back much further: back to the Creation. When Adam and Eve disobeyed God this curse was put on all mankind. What was the curse? Simple. Hard work! Instead of living in a Garden of Eden where everything was provided for them people would now have to "struggle to scratch a living from it (the earth)."

Have you ever made the statement: "Nothing comes easy any more?" I have. In this complex 21st Century world we live in it seems like everything is difficult. Just calling a business to obtain information is usually fraught with an array of choices you must make before you can even talk to a real person. It's work. It requires patience.

We must work for a living. Work is the curse that we live under but work is also a blessing. Ask anyone who has been out of work for a while or someone who is physically unable to perform a job, and they will tell you how blessed you are to be able to work. Retirees who have worked hard all their lives and enjoyed their job until age required them to give it up often think back to their "working days" with fondness.

Work may be the curse we live under, but it is one that we are blessed to have. The harder we work and the more we accomplish the greater is our self satisfaction and the closer we are to God. After all He has designated "work" as the thing we do to be successful in life.

No matter if the 2005 White Sox were closer to stooges than superstars it was their hard work that overcame the curse and made them champions.

Big Inning Baseball Quote #64:

Breaking a curse gives baseball players multiple reputations:

"A ballplayer has two reputations, one with the other players and one with the fans. The first is based on ability. The second the newspapers give him."

---Johnny Evers---
Chicago Cubs
World Series Champs 1906-07

Diamond Lesson #65

Pennant Race

Remember that in a race everyone runs, but only one person gets the prize. You also must run in such a way that you will win. **1 Corinthians 9:24**

Tom Seaver, Hall of Fame pitcher, said it best. "There are only two places in this league. First place and no place." Moral victories and "wait-'til-next-year" mentality are for losers. The only statistic that is meaningful in the end is games won.

A pennant is a narrow tapered flag. That's what the teams get to fly above their stadium denoting they are league champs. The pennant winners in the National League then square off against the pennant winning American League team. So, when the bell rings on opening day the pennant race is on. Racking up wins to begin with doesn't assure the pennant but it makes the road less difficult at the end.

In the majors the pennant race starts in the spring and ends in the fall. It covers 162 games. If you win enough of those games, you get to play more. The pennant race is followed by the League Championship Series and the World Series.

This pennant race is a long haul. Sometimes the race gets out of hand early. If a first place team gets a big lead then interest wanes. The die-hard fans never give up. They will always recall the Giants of 1951 who trailed the Dodgers by 13 and ½ games, but kept on playing hard and overtook them, forcing a playoff. Then came the "Shot Heard 'Round the World," Bobby Thomson's dramatic pennant winning home run. The World Series was anticlimactic.

There have been other great pennant races. Remember the 1915 Federal League race? Me neither, but it was a doozy. They had a five-team race until mid-September. Pittsburgh, St. Louis, Kansas City, Chicago, and Newark battled until the final weekend. St. Louis won the most games including a final day doubleheader, but Chicago won the pennant by .001 percentage points. Two postponed games had not been made up and league rules didn't stipulate that they had to be made up after the season ended. So Chicago…not the Cubs or White Sox…but the Whales won the pennant.

Only one team gets the prize. That's the story in any race. 1 Corinthians 9:24 says that every runner in the race is running, but only one will win. It is important to train hard to be ready for the race. It is even more important to run hard for the entire race.

You've often heard it said that life is a journey. If we train hard and watch our health we have a chance to live to a ripe old age. It is not a 100-yard dash but more like a marathon run. On a long run there is a greater opportunity to get knocked off course by the many distractions that come along and not to finish the race the way we intended.

Winning any race is hard work. It takes self-discipline. Paul points out that the Christian life requires not only hard work, but self-denial and grueling preparation. We can't win by observing. We can't just jog a couple of laps and expect to win. We must be diligent in our training.

The NLT says, "The essential disciplines of prayer, Bible study, and worship equip us to run with vigor and stamina." By constantly putting these into practice we stay the course. We are able to beat off any distractions that would knock us off course. Our eyes are on the prize and we fully intend to win God's pennant race.

215

Big Inning Baseball Quote #65:

It takes perseverance to win a pennant:

If you do everything right every day you will still lose 40% of your games—but you'll also end up in the World Series.

**Thomas Boswell
author, The Heart of the Order (1989)**

Diamond Lesson #66

Southpaw

John's clothes were woven from camel hair and he wore a leather belt; his food was locusts and wild honey.   Matthew 3:4-5

In the old ballpark in Chicago back around 1885, when a pitcher was standing on the pitcher's mound his left arm was facing the south. This was so the batter would be facing east and would not have the afternoon or evening sun in his eyes. Thus, left-handers became known as southpaws. I'm sure there are other theories about how that term came about but this is the one we will accept because it is different and southpaws are different.

There is kind of a myth surrounding left-handed pitchers. It is thought their pitches move more than a right-hander's. Still, righties have pitched 75% of the major leagues' no-hitters.   Why are lefties viewed differently? Maybe it's just their way of thinking? Lefty Gomez was called "Goofy" because of his antics. Once when his catcher came to the mound to ask what pitch he wanted to throw a tough hitter Gomez said, "I don't want to throw him nothing. Maybe he'll get tired of waiting and leave."

A modern day version of Gomez was Bill "Spaceman" Lee who pitched 14 years in the majors with Boston and Montreal. Lee had an interesting take on left handedness that refuted any theories about southpaws being crazy. "There are two hemispheres in our brain—a left and a right. The left hemisphere controls the right side or your body and the right hemisphere controls the left side. It's a fact. Therefore, lefthanders are the only people in their right minds."

Who can argue with that? As Tommy John said, "The good Lord smiled on me when he gave me left handed genes." Yes, Southpaws are different.

An important person in the Bible was considered different. We don't have any information to indicate that John the Baptist was a southpaw, but he was considered odd. Maybe that's what caused people to listen when he spoke. God had entrusted him with a very important role. He was to be the forerunner who announced the coming of the Messiah. His message was loud and clear. "There is One coming who is greater than me."

John resided in the wilderness. According to *Nelson's Bible Dictionary* the wilderness was a "vast badland of crags, wind, and heat." The Israelites knew about the wilderness. Remember they had wandered in it for 40 years before God led them into the Promised Land. So John called the people away from the comfort of their homes out into the wilderness where they could be closer to God.

And when they got out there he told them about Jesus. He baptized them symbolizing "moral regeneration." Dressed in camel hair, eating wild locusts and honey, John presented an unusual sight. His wild appearance alone was enough to get their attention. Then he hit home with his message. He told them that just because they were the children of Abraham not to consider themselves secure with God and think they could live anyway they wanted to.   He said the One who was coming would show them how to live. He would give them hope and the secure future they were seeking. John the Baptist's Southpaw approach to things won many over to Christianity.

Big Inning Baseball Quote #66

When this southpaw's fastball spoke, batter's listened.

"Pitching is the art of instilling fear."

--Sandy Koufax—
Hall of Fame Southpaw

Diamond Lesson #67

College World Series

But, seek first His kingdom and His righteousness and all these things will be given to you as well.   Matthew 6:33

My first trip to the College World Series was in 1986 as a member of the radio broadcast team for the Florida State Seminoles. I didn't know what to expect. Thought I might be back home after two games. I ended up staying 11 days as FSU made it all the way to the championship game before losing to Arizona in the 40th NCAA College World Series. It was quite an experience!

There is something magical about the CWS. Although Omaha, Nebraska, is hardly the most exciting town in America, it is at World Series time. People from all over the country descended on Johnny Rosenblatt Stadium, named after the Omaha mayor who first got the CWS to come to Omaha in 1950, where it has found a permanent home. The first two series had been played in Kalamazoo, Michigan ('47-'48) and number three was contested in Wichita, Kansas in 1949. It's a sign of the times that after 60 years in Rosenblatt in 2011 the CWS moved to the new TD Ameritrade Park.

It was a money-losing event for the first twelve years but nobody cared. This represented the ultimate in college baseball. In 1980 ESPN began to televise the CWS and its popularity accelerated. In 1991 CBS added CWS games to its programming. Thanks to these two networks, college players could receive the same national attention the major leaguers got. It was good for the college game.

Television changed the format to create even more excitement. The eight-team format was divided into two four-team double elimination brackets. The bracket winners then played a two out of three championship round.

The College World Series presents a unique platform for college players that has catapulted many of them into the major leagues. Stars like Roger Clemens, Barry Bonds, and Bob Horner made it big after their college baseball days. There was another guy who fared pretty well after playing in the 1948 CWS with Yale: future president George H. W. Bush was the Eli's first baseman in the Series.

As any college baseball coach will tell his players, you must first do the little things right, before you get to the College World Series. You have to win regular season, regional and super-regional games before you make it to Omaha. Jesus advised the same thing in Matthew 6 when he said to seek the kingdom first.

Taking care of business is the way that you achieve the ultimate victory. We don't need to worry so much about being able to do these little things that we don't make it to the big show. Jesus said don't worry about the trivialities like what you're going to wear and what you will eat. The way you live your life is more important than that because your heavenly Father will look out for you in these things.

After all, "see the lilies in the field. They don't labor or spin." Yet they are arrayed even more beautifully than King Solomon. Look at the birds. "They do not sow or reap or store in barns." But look how God takes care of them.

So, quit worrying. You can't add a single hour to your life by worrying. When your time is up it is up. We need to focus on doing the things that grow God's kingdom.

We do that by concentrating less on ourselves and our plans and more on God's plans for our lives.

Jesus closes by saying: "Don't worry about tomorrow, it has enough trouble of its own." So take care of today. Win those games and you'll end up in the real World Series-the Heavenly One.

Big Inning Baseball Quote #67:

It's all about winning, but doggone it, you're going to lose some too.

"No matter how good you are, you're going to lose a third of your games. No matter how bad you are, you're going to win a third of your game. It's the other third that makes the difference."

---Tommy LaSorda---

Diamond Lesson #68

Batting Practice

With the measure you use it will be measured to you and even more.   **Mark 4:24**

As any baseball fan knows— B.P.— means batting practice. The most die hard fans, as well as those traffic beaters who arrive at the ball park early, are able to watch the sluggers knock those BP fastballs into the stands.

The purpose of batting practice is to enable the hitters to get their muscles loosened up and their swings grooved. It's not about the pitcher or it would be called pitching practice. Since they are out to fine tune the batter's pre-game approach it is called batting practice.

The BP pitcher is not a member of the pitching staff. He's usually a coach or former pitcher. His job is to make the pitches hittable, not to fool the batter. Hence, he throws lots of fastballs and only utilizes breaking pitches when he forewarns the batter or when the batter requests one.

Consequently, you'll sometimes hear an announcer say that a batter hit a "BP fastball" for a home run. He would be describing a subpar pitch that lacked movement The decision a batter has to make to hit the ball in BP is substantially different from the amount of time he has to pull the trigger during a game.

Motivational speaker Phil Steffen, in a talk entitled "You think you have to make quick decisions?" says: "The next time you complain about having to make important decisions too quickly, consider this: A fastball leaves a baseball pitcher's hand at around 90 miles per hour, traveling 55 feet in about 4/10 of a second. The batter has about

2/10ths of a second to decide whether or not to swing. The ball is in the right position for a batter to hit it for only two feet of its journey to the catcher's mitt, or about 15/100th of a second. So how much time do you have for your decision?" Obviously a batter has a lot more time to decide to hit a BP fastball than a game pitch. When viewed in that light maybe some of our snap decisions don't have to be made as quickly as we think.

Life is full of decisions. Some require immediate attention. On others we can take our time, study all the options, and decide what to do. The latter is what Jesus is referring to in Mark 4 when he says" *Consider carefully what you hear. With the measure that you use, it will be measured to you---and even more.*

When a light shines on an object its natural beauty as well as its imperfections are revealed. Jesus is saying that He has revealed His truth to us through His teachings and it is up to us to consider what we have heard and to act upon it. We may not understand this fully. There may be something blocking our ability to perceive His truth. Maybe we understand some, but not all of it.

The more we attempt to learn by studying His Word and through prayer and obedience, the more of the truth is revealed to us. As the NLT Bible says, "The truth is clear, but our ability to understand is imperfect. As we obey, we will sharpen our vision and increase our understanding. As we learn we make better decisions."

A batter who sees and recognizes a pitch still has something to do. He must swing the bat. If he doesn't swing and it's a strike, he can be called out. Likewise during our at-bats on earth we will be judged by how we recognize the truth and act upon it. We don't want to be called out at home plate.

Big Inning Baseball Quote #68:

This batter was feared by pitchers, even before the game:

"I was such a dangerous hitter I even got intentional walks during batting practice."

---Casey Stengel---

Diamond Lesson #69

Scroogie

Look straight ahead and fix your eyes on what lies before you. Mark out a straight path for your feet; then stick to the path and stay safe.   Proverbs 4:25-26

"There's a pitch in baseball called a screwball, perfected by a pitcher named Carl Hubbell back in the 1930's. It's a pitch with a particular spin that sort of flutters and drops, goes in different directions and behaves in very unexpected ways..." Andrew Bergman used that description of a baseball pitch to describe what he called "Screwball Comedies," i.e. crazy movies. Some of the ones he referred to were "It Happened One Night" with Clark Gable and Claudette Colbert; "The Thin Man" starring William Powell and Myrna Loy; and "His Girl Friday" with Cary Grant and Rosalind Russell.

Those "screwball" movies would seem tame by current standards. And the screwball may not be as unique as it once was in baseball, but it is still a very effective pitch when thrown properly. How does the inventor of the pitch, often called the "scroogie" describe it? "The screwball's an unnatural pitch. Nature never intended man to turn his hand like that, like throwing rocks at a bear," said Hubbell.

Not a lot of pitchers throw a screwball for several reasons. First of all, it is hard on the arm. When the screwball is released the pitcher has to snap his wrist sharply inward which puts a lot of strain on the forearm. The forearm has to be rotated about 90 degrees in. But, if you can do all that, control it and not hurt yourself you've got one heckuva pitch.

The main thing that makes a screwball difficult to hit is the different rotation it has. When a right-handed batter starts to stride into a screwball from a right-handed

227

pitcher, he finds the ball breaking sharply in on his wrists. It's a good pitch for getting popups or weak grounders. For a left-handed batter it looks more like a curveball and breaks away from him. Not many can throw the screwball well, but those who can have a unique pitch in their arsenal.

When we start to pursue the unnatural or the screwball things in life we run into difficulty just like an untrained pitcher trying to throw a scroogie. Proverbs 4:25-26 cautions us to "look straight ahead" and to walk on "level paths" that are firm to your feet.

This must be where we get the phrase "stay on the straight and narrow." When we do that we avoid things that will trip us up. If you stay on the path that is solid and is going the right way, you avoid those roots and briars and quicksand and other unpleasant things that make life more difficult.

There's lots of stuff going on away from the "straight and narrow" that can be tempting. The Message says, "Keep your eyes straight ahead; ignore all sideshow distractions." It's obvious that when we stay focused on where we are going we are more likely to get there than if we take an unknown, indirect route. After all, if we get off the main route we may bump into a bunch of screwballs out there and we know what a lack of success hitters have against the scroogie. Better to follow Solomon's advice in Proverbs and stay on the level ground of that straight and narrow path.

Big Inning Baseball Quote #69:

Talk about a screwball, this guy was an original:

"When you're a winner you're always happy, but if you're happy as a loser you'll always be a loser."

---Mark Fidrych—
Tigers Pitcher

Diamond Lesson #70

No Cryin' in Baseball

I lie in the dust, completely discouraged; revive me by your word.   *Psalm 119:25*

"I was just wonderin' why you would throw home when we got a two run lead. You let the tying run get on second base and we lost the lead because of you. Start using your head," manager Jimmy Dugan (Tom Hanks) confronted his centerfielder Evelyn Gardner when she returned to the dugout during a scene in the movie "A League of their Own."

Whereupon, Evelyn started to cry which prompted this now famous line from Hanks. "Are you crying? Are you crying? ARE YOU CRYING? There's no crying. There's no crying in baseball."

Okay, so it was a fictional all-girls professional baseball team and it was only a movie. Is there crying in real baseball? Well, maybe it would read better if it was written there is no crying for baseball. Gosh, look at the money those guys make nowadays.

In 2005, the average Major League Salary was $2,349,394. If there was crying in baseball I guess the loudest wails would have come from the Big Apple. The New York Yankees who were eliminated in the first round of the playoffs paid out $207,152,931 to achieve that. The New York Mets had the third highest payroll. They shelled out $103, 985,823 to finish tied for third in their division. And the Boston Redsox paid a second best or worst, $116,640, 070, to not defend their world championship successfully.

There was certainly no crying on the south side of Chicago where the World Champion White Sox were down in the middle of the salary pack (13th) paying only

$73,162, 000. Maybe the crying in Chicago would come in 2006 when all those champions asked for big raises.

Look ahead 10 years to see who is set up for a crying jag. Starting the 2015 season the Dodgers payroll is over $272 million and the Yankees are paying out almost $220 mil. Both teams watched the Giants and Royals play in the 2014 World Series. The Redsox who finished last in 2014 standings rank 3rd in 2015 payroll with upwards of $187 mil. Yes, there was potential for crying in baseball in the 2015 season.

In defeat we feel like crying. Maybe the bills are piling up and the commissions are not coming in. Perhaps there are family illnesses to deal with. Maybe the job pressures are piling up.   Sometimes we sympathize with the Psalmist who wrote "I lie in the dust completely discouraged; revive me by your word."   The same scripture (PS. 119:25) in The Message reads: "I'm feeling terrible—couldn't feel worse! Get me on my feet again. You promised, remember?"

The Psalmist is referring to the promises that are contained in God's word. There is power in the word. It is restorative power. It does lift us up and put us back on track. That's what the Psalmist was seeking in these verses. Remember the old hymn: "There is power, power, wonder working power in the name (word) of the Lord."

God's word is what we turn to for guidance through the tough times because his power is revealed through it. When the game is on the line, the bases are loaded, and we're only up by a run, we need this wonder-working power. Sure, there is crying in life, even if there is no crying in baseball but crying is not the final answer. God hears our cries and sees our tears. He stands ready to help us when we seek his help. Reading His word, praying, worshipping, those are the things He provides us with so we can communicate with Him. They keep down the crying in life and in baseball.

Big Inning Baseball Quote #70:

There was crying in this baseball town.

"Oh somewhere in this favored land the sun is shining bright;
The band is playing somewhere, and somewhere hearts are light,
And somewhere men are laughing, and somewhere children shout
But, there is no joy in Mudville. Mighty Casey has struck out."

**---Casey at the Bat—
Baseball's most famous poem
by Ernest Lawrence Thayer
1st printed in 1888**

Diamond Lesson #71

20-Game Winner

But the one who received the seed that fell on good soil is the man who hears the word and understands it. He produces a crop, yielding a hundred, sixty or thirty times what was sown. Matthew 13:23

There are certain benchmarks that indicate excellence in your field when they are achieved. For pitchers, one of those is winning 20 games in a season. It is such a magical plateau that former pitcher Jim Bouton wrote in his classic book *Ball Four,* "If you had a pill that would guarantee a pitcher twenty wins, but might take five years off his life, he would take it."

Warren Spahn (Braves) and Christy Mathewson (Giants) both won 20 games in a NL record 13 seasons. Walter Johnson (Senators) hit the mark in 12 years to lead all AL pitchers. They just don't make 'em like that any more. Spahn retired in 1963; Mathewson in 1916; and Johnson in 1927.

That's not to say there aren't some great pitchers around these days. They just don't complete games that often. In an age of specialists, not many starters are around to care-take their victory at the end of the game. Sometimes those victories turn into defeats in the hands of the relief corps. For example, Hall-of-Famer Nolan Ryan whose career strikeouts— 5,714— eclipses all others, only won 20+ in two seasons: 1973-74, with the Angels. In those two years he had the most complete games of his career, 26 each season. He did not win 20 games in a season for the remaining 20 years of his 27-year career.

Perhaps, the most amazing feat of winning 20 games rests with the 1971 Baltimore Orioles. They had an unheard of 4-20 game winners on the same staff: Jim

234

Palmer, Dave McNally, Mike Cuellar, and Pat Dobson. The Orioles won the pennant easily, but did not win the World Series. While winning 20 games is memorable it does not ensure the ultimate prize in baseball---becoming World Champions.

Twenty game winners are those pitchers who develop the talents they are given to the fullest extent. Jesus talked about using the talents we are given in the 13th Chapter of Matthew. Here's the way *The Message* puts it:

> *Study this story of the farmer planting seed. When anyone hears news of the kingdom and doesn't take it in, it just remains on the surface, and so the Evil One comes along and plucks it right out of that person's heart. This is the seed the farmer scatters on the road.*
> *The seed cast in the gravel—this is the person who hears and instantly responds with enthusiasm. But, there is no soil of character, and so when the emotions wear off and some difficulty arrives, there is nothing to show for it.*
> *The seed cast in the weeds is the person who hears the kingdom news, but weeds of worry and illusions about getting more and wanting everything under the sun strangle what was heard, and nothing comes of it.*
> *The seed cast on good earth is the person who hears and takes in the News, and then produces a harvest beyond his wildest dreams.*

Seeds grow quietly and persistently. They don't create a lot of hoopla or hype. They just do the job they were planted to do. Their results can only be as good as the soil they were planted in. The soil represents our lives and how we receive all kinds of usable as well as non-usable material. The seed, representing our talents and abilities is a gift. What we do with it is up to us. Will we be like the gravel, the weeds or the road where the seeds didn't grow? Or will we work hard to develop our gift and do as Jesus pointed out in the parable: "The one who hears and does the things he is supposed to will multiply those talents into a yield of 100, 60 or 30 times what was sown." Now that even beats being a 20 game winner.

Big Inning Baseball Quote #71:

A unique way to use those talents, but it worked:

"I always aimed for the middle of the plate. I knew the ball wasn't going to be there

 anyway."

---Jim Palmer---
Baltimore Orioles

Diamond Lesson #72

Diving Catch

Whatever you do, work at it with all your heart as working for the Lord, not for men.
Colossians 3:23

It was the top of the fifth inning, there were two men on base with two outs and the score was tied. Okay so this was a June game, it wasn't like the pennant was riding on this one play. The Angels were playing the Royals in a mid-season AL matchup. Ho hum! But listen to what happened.

USATODAY.com says David Howard (not a household name) was at the plate. Out in centerfield Jim Edmonds was playing shallow. Then, "Howard lined a shot to straightaway center. Edmonds turned his back to home plate and took off running (full speed), then dove, fully extending his body horizontal to the ground, and caught the ball over his shoulder. He landed on the warning track a few feet from the wall." Like I said, the season wasn't on the line, but that's the way Edmonds plays every day.

Really, how good was that catch? Well, usually an umpire doesn't comment on baseball plays. After all they see good catches all the time. But later veteran umpire Dave Phillips, told the *Kansas City Star,* "That was one of the greatest catches ever. That made Willie Mays' play look routine." (see Diamond Lesson #8: *Highlight Film Catch*)

A diving catch that did have a lot on the line and really left a player open to injury occurred in the 2005 World Series. The White Sox fans were sitting on pins and needles as a tight pitchers duel against the Astros took the fourth game into the 9th inning. The Sox leading the series, three games to none, needed just three outs to preserve a 1-0 win. Could they get them and win their first World Series in 88 years?

237

With the tying run on second pinch hitter Chris Burke, who had killed the Braves' hopes with a home run in the playoffs, lifted a foul ball that was headed for the stands. Sox shortstop Juan Uribe was headed full tilt that way. With complete disregard for his own safety he banged into the rail, reached into the stands and made a backhand catch. Then he fell into the seats among the fans. Uribe's diving catch had saved the series clincher for the Whitesox.

Jim Edmonds and Juan Uribe as well as many others who have made diving catches were going all out for victory. They were playing with heart. We are instructed to perform "heartily" as if we are working for the Lord not for men.

There are lots of tasks that seem routine and a lot of them aren't that enjoyable to perform. We often try to avoid doing them. But, any task, no matter how lowly it may seem, can be elevated to one of importance if we work as if working for the Lord and not for man.

So as the *Believer's Bible Commentary (pg. 2015) says:* "In this sense, there is no difference between secular and sacred work. All is sacred. Rewards in heaven will not be for prominence or apparent successes; they will not be for talents or opportunities; but rather for faithfulness."

So, we don't have to be superstars to make great plays. All we have to do is to have the proper approach to everything we do. It doesn't matter if we are waiting tables, cleaning house, parking cars, mowing lawns, or reading bedtime stories. Whenever we commit what we are doing to the Lord and work for Him then our task is elevated above the mundane. It becomes the equivalent of a diving catch for the Lord.

Big Inning Baseball Quote #72:

The master of great catches:

"He's not at his locker yet, but four guys are over there interviewing his glove."

---Rex Barney---
on Brooks Robinson

Diamond Lesson #73

Changeup

All who heard him were amazed. "Isn't this the same man who persecuted Jesus' followers with such devastation in Jerusalem?" **Acts 9:21**

"The changeup is the second most important pitch," says former FSU pitching coach Jamey Shouppe, current Florida A&M head coach. "The best pitch in baseball is a well located fast ball. If you can throw that then the changeup is an excellent pitch to have."

The premise behind the changeup is that it looks like something else causing the hitter to adjust too late to hit it well. It is thrown with the same arm speed as the fastball, but because of the way it is held and released the rotation takes some of the speed off of the ball.

The two most common changeups are the straight change and the circle change. The straight change is held with three fingers instead of two and is closer to the palm of the hand. It will usually break a little downward. Shouppe says they call that changeup a BP (batting practice) fastball. It usually comes in around 75 mph. He seldom teaches that to his pitchers.

The one he likes is the circle change. The pitchers Shouppe teaches the circle change can have different movement on the pitch depending on the finger placements on the ball. The most common grip is to form a circle with the index finger and the thumb, using these two fingers to grip the seams of the baseball. It's a pitch that Pedro Martinez used very effectively throughout his career.

Shouppe says that very few pitchers come to college with a changeup in their arsenal. He calls it a "feel" pitch. "The first week we teach it to a new pitcher he is sure he can't throw it. The second week, he says maybe it has possibilities. The third week he begins to feel like he can throw it." Those who mastered this pitch at Florida State were usually the ones who made it into the starting rotation and became successful.

The apostle Paul experienced a great change in his life that has effected the scriptures ever since. Paul was a zealot. A man who never did anything halfway. He always went full speed ahead. He was a Roman citizen and one of the most avid persecutors of those who proclaimed the Christian faith until one day on the road to Damascus when God struck him blind. That got Paul's attention.

After God restored his sight, Paul became not only a believer, but one of the most dynamic preachers of the word. He went on three missionary journeys throughout the Roman Empire preaching for Christ. His letters to the churches he had visited form much of the New Testament.

Before Paul's conversion those who were Christians would flee when they knew he was in the territory. When he returned after his conversion experience he had a different story to tell. He was a brilliant scholar and was always able to argue his points powerfully. His talks got people's attention.

Now what caught their attention was Paul's changed life and his new message. Paul lived what he spoke. People could see that he really believed what he was talking about because it showed in his life. Paul used a changeup in his life effectively to make a lasting statement for Christianity.

Big Inning Baseball Quote #73:

Changeup had a different meaning for this guy:

"Ruth made a grave mistake when he gave up pitching. Working once a week, he might have lasted a long time and become a great star."

---Tris Speaker---
about the Babe

Diamond Lesson #74

Million-Dollar Catch, Dime-Throw

Other seed fell on shallow soil with underlying rock. This seed began to grow, but soon it withered and died for lack of moisture.   Luke 8:6

Brett Groves, former Florida State shortstop, went deep into the hole and made a super backhanded catch to stop a certain base hit. Then, he threw the ball low and it skipped past the first baseman enabling the batter to end up on second base. Instead of a highlight film play it ended up a two base throwing error or as Brett's Dad, Tom, used to call it a "million-dollar catch and a dime throw."

This is not to demean Groves as a player because he had an excellent college career and went on to become a steady professional player, but it points out something that happens a lot in sports. When a player doesn't complete a play, instead of a great play it turns out being a worse situation than if the play hadn't been made at all. In the above example, instead of getting a single if Groves hadn't made the play, the batter ends up in scoring position on a two-base throwing error.

Sometimes it's just a case of trying to be too spectacular. In basketball for example you might see a player make an outstanding steal, take off with the ball at full speed, hurry his slam dunk and bang it off the rim instead of scoring. Or he might try to add a world class pass off the remarkable steal instead of settling things down and throw the ball away, thereby negating a great effort.

In baseball, sometimes it is better just to hold the ball after making a great catch rather than hurrying the throw and making an error. This is especially true when there are men on base. Like making a diving catch to keep a ball from going through the infield, then trying to throw behind the runner and throwing it away enabling the runner to score anyway. Sometimes a player just has to settle for the million-dollar catch and avoid the dime throw.

Returning to Jesus' parable of the soil and the seeds there is a message that fits in with the million-dollar catch and dime throw in baseball. The baseball scenario demonstrates a situation that looks like it is going to be great, but turns out to be disappointing.

Jesus is telling the story of the farmer sowing seeds and how not every seed falls in the best place to obtain growth. That is the case with the seed that falls in an area where there is rock in the soil. It looks like the seed might begin to grow. But the rock keeps it from getting any moisture and it soon dies. What first looked promising ends in disappointment for the sower of the seed that falls on rocky ground.

In this parable Jesus is talking about those who hear the word of God and how they react to it. Those who hear His word, but don't let the message get through to them and impact their lives in a positive manner are likened to seed on rocky ground. The seed can only penetrate so far, but it can't take root. Then because the rocks are preventing the life-giving moisture, the seed never grows. It simply dies.

Jesus is warning us against those million dollar catches and dime throws in life. He wants us to complete each action and turn it into a positive deed. When we read the Bible or attend a church service, hear the message, but do nothing with it we are doing the same thing as a fielder who makes a great catch, but negates it with a bad throw.

Big Inning Baseball Quote #74:

You make some good ones and some bad ones:

"Some days you tame the tiger. And some days the tiger has you for lunch."

---Tug McGraw—
about relief pitching

Diamond Lesson #75

Batter's Box

Commit thy works unto the Lord and thy thoughts shall be established.   Proverbs 16:3

Stepping into the batter's box signals a commitment. MLB Rule 6.02: "The batter shall take his position in the batter's box promptly when it is his time to hit. The batter shall not leave his position in the batter's box after the pitcher comes to a set position or starts his windup."

Of course there are two batter's boxes. One is for right handed batters the other is for left handed swingers. Once the batter is in the box the only way he can get out without experiencing a penalty, i.e. a called strike, is to request timeout. The umpire usually will grant the batter's wish and then he can step out of the box.

All of that is elementary for those who follow baseball. The players know the rules. They can't call timeout or step out of the batter's box while the pitcher is getting ready to throw. A batter is not allowed to try to distract the pitcher while he's in the batter's box, nor can the pitcher deceive the batter with any false motions.

There are other happenings that enable the batter to step out of the box other than calling time. Those are:

1. After he swings at a pitch

2. If he's forced out of the box by a pitch

3. Someone else calls time

4. A defensive player attempts a play on a base runner

5. He attempts a bunt

6. A wild pitch, passed ball, or balk occurs

7. The pitcher leaves the pitching mound after receiving the ball.

8. The catcher leaves the box to give signals.

Other than those reasons the batter is committed to hitting once he steps in the batter's box and must stay there.

King Solomon, the wisest king to rule over Israel, talked about commitment in Proverbs. Solomon knew that the best way to insure that dreams and goals would be achieved was to commit your work to the Lord.

J. Allen Blair wrote: "Occasionally we find ourselves disturbed and depressed, even in trying to do the Lord's work. Could anything be further from what God desires? God cannot work through anxious hearts. Whenever a Christian reaches this state, he should stop at once and ask himself, 'Whose work is it?' If it's God's work, never forget the burden of it is His, too. You are not the important person. Christ is! He is at work through us. What should we do then when things do not go well? Go to Him! Anything less than this is disobedience." (see *Believer's Bible Commentary* pg. 831)

We are told to commit our work to God. The nice thing about doing that is when we step into the batter's box then this commitment to work becomes His problem. Since you have dedicated it to God, it is His responsibility to see you through it. That is what He has promised and that is what He will do!

Big Inning Baseball Quote #75:

Talk about a player who knew what to do in the batter's box:

"One of these days he will hit the ball so hard it will burst and all he will get for his effort is a single."

                         ---Casey Stengel---
                         on Mickey Mantle

Diamond Lesson #76

Fat Pitch

"You will not surely die," the serpent said to the woman. For God knows that when you eat of it your eyes will be opened, and you will be like God, knowing good and evil."   **Genesis 3:4-5**

It's going, going, gone! That's usually what you'll hear an announcer say when a pitcher delivers a fat pitch. Often a fat pitch will sail off of the bat and out of the ballpark. A fat pitch is a very hittable pitch. It's usually right over the plate. Definitely a mistake that a pitcher doesn't want to make.

Other names you might hear used to describe a fat pitch include: room service; meatball; cream puff; lollipop; grapefruit; pumpkin; and cookie. All terms that are favorable to a hitter not the pitcher.

A fat pitch is a pitching coach's worst nightmare. He goes to great lengths to figure out how to aid his pitchers in avoiding the delivery of one. Dave Duncan, former pitching coach of the St. Louis Cardinals, tracked every pitch that his pitchers made. He took those charts with him everywhere…maybe he even slept with them.

In the book, *Three Nights in August,* author Buzz Bissinger explained what was on Duncan's charts. "He has noted not only every pitch, but who threw it to whom and what that batter did with it. Duncan tries to uncover any trends that can be spotted in particular situations. Duncan wants to know how many first pitch hits have been given up as opposed to the number of first pitch outs recorded and what kinds of pitches have caused these results."

"He also wants to know when two strike hits have occurred; on what pitches and in what part of the game and in what situations. Duncan looks at the two out and two strike pitches. Everything he can study that will enable him to assist his pitchers is on those charts. In addition he is continually watching edited videos of his pitchers in action. Dave Duncan goes the extra mile to help his pitchers avoid throwing the fat pitch."

Just as Duncan tried to increase a pitcher's knowledge there is an example where a quest for information in the Bible caused problems that we still feel the results of today. This information came out of disobedience to God. Because of it sin was introduced into a perfect world.

We learn from Genesis that when God created man and woman he put them in a perfect setting. Adam and Eve were situated in the Garden of Eden where He took care of all of their needs. They weren't overburdened with a bunch of rules either. God had only given them one commandment.

God surrounded them with all sorts of beautiful trees with delicious fruits. Adam and Eve had their pick with one exception. The big tree in the middle was not to be eaten from. "He told them not to eat from the tree of the knowledge of good and evil." Why would Adam and Eve need to know about good and evil any way? They lived in a perfect, problem-free world. They only had to obey one commandment and they blew it.

Satan, disguised as a serpent, tempted Eve to eat of the tree and she fell for it. He used the kind of logic that goes with wrong thinking. Surely God didn't mean what He said. Look at that fruit. See how good it looks. So Eve disobeyed and so did Adam.

Satan threw a curve ball, disguised as a fat pitch, and sin entered the world. Nothing would come easy after that for all of mankind.

Big Inning Baseball Quote #76:

Maybe this is a case of too many fat pitches:

"I had most of my trouble with left-handed hitters. Charlie Gehringer could hit me in a tunnel at midnight with the lights out."

---Lefty Gomez---

Diamond Lesson #77

Monuments

Peter blurted out, Lord this is wonderful. If you want me to, I'll make three shrines, one for you, one for Moses, and one for Elijah.   Matthew 17:4

He went to Columbia University on a football scholarship, but became one of the most famous names in baseball history. His number "4" jersey was the first one to be retired in American sports. Lou Gehrig, "the Iron Horse," didn't miss a day of work in 17 years despite 17 fractures in his hands, being beaned several times, suffering through minor illnesses, having severe back pain and some other minor injuries. With a lifetime batting average of .340, with 493 homers and 1,995 RBI, a monument commemorates Gehrig's career and life.

Monument Park at Yankee Stadium has the most well known collection of monuments of any baseball park. In fact, it was the first baseball field to be designated as a stadium. It was transported over to the new Yankee Stadium in 2009. The first monument was placed in the field of play, in front of the flagpole in centerfield. It was dedicated on May 30, 1932, to Miller Huggins who managed in NY from 1918 to 1929.

Gehrig became the first player to have a monument dedicated to him on July 6, 1941. Eight years later Babe Ruth's monument was erected. At that time, Babe, Lou, and Miller had the only three monuments located in centerfield 450 feet from home plate.

According to Wikipedia, the on-line dictionary, Casey Stengel was watching his outfielder fumble a ball around near the monuments in a game once and shouted out: "Ruth, Gehrig, Huggins, *somebody* get that ball back to the infield."

Joe Dimaggio and Mickey Mantle were awarded plaques that later were replaced by monuments. Those five monuments are the main attractions of the Yankees monument park that also has many plaques commemorating New York baseball heroes.

The dictionary definition of a monument is: "Something set up to keep alive the memory of a person or event, as a tablet, statue, pillar, building, etc." The idea of building monuments to honor people is ancient. We find references to it in the Bible.

One of the more famous ones, that didn't actually come about, is found on the Mount of Transfiguration. Jesus took Peter, James and John up on a high mountain. As Matthew 17:2 explains: "As the men watched, Jesus' appearance changed so that His face shone like the sun and His clothes became dazzling white. Suddenly, Moses and Elijah appeared and began talking with Jesus."

You can imagine how dumbfounded the three disciples must have been. Not only to see the change in appearance of Jesus, which was certainly brought about by the hand of God, but to see two of the legends of Jewish history.

Peter was always a man of action or, as John MacArthur describes him in his book *Twelve Ordinary Men,* "eager, aggressive, bold, and outspoken—with a habit of revving his mouth while his brain was in neutral." Naturally he thought action was called for on this monumental occasion. He would build three monuments (shrines). Makes sense doesn't it? Not really. Even as Peter blurted out, "Lord this is wonderful. If you want me too I'll make three shrines," a bright cloud appeared and God spoke saying this was His Beloved Son, in whom He was well-pleased. No need for a monument here. God had spoken. That's all that was needed to commemorate the event!

Big Inning Baseball Quote #77:

A guy who was truly deserving of a monument:

"…you have been reading about the bad break I got. Yet, today I consider myself the luckiest man on the face of this earth. I've been in ballparks for 17 years and have never received anything but kindness and encouragement from you fans…So, I close in saying I may have had a tough break, but I have an awful lot to live for."

---Lou Gehrig---
farewell speech

Diamond Lesson #78

Great Day to Play Two

This is the day the Lord has made. Let us be glad and rejoice in it. **Psalm 118:24**

"It's a beautiful day for a ballgame. Let's play two." That saying was made famous by Mr. Cub, Ernie Banks. Never on a pennant contender in 19 seasons of playing the game, all in Chicago, it was Banks' love of the game that prompted him to say that. He was always ready to play.

In 19 seasons encompassing 2,528 games, Ernie Banks never played in a post-season game. The Cubs were seldom even in contention for the pennant. Still he won the League's MVP award twice, 1958 & 1959. It was his love of the game that enabled him to excel and not be able to get enough of the game.

Actor Joe Mantegna, who has appeared in over 60 movies, is a Chicago native and a lifelong, long-suffering Cubs fan. Here's his assessment of Ernie Banks, "He never complained about his team's bad luck or bad talent, never stopped playing the game with joy, never stopped giving his all, never lost his proud demeanor, and never acted like anything but a winner. He was a symbol of the Cub fans' undiminishing resilience. If he could be happy to come to the park each afternoon, then so could we."

Banks speaks for baseball fans everywhere who just love being at the ballpark. They may fight the traffic to get to the ball park; have a long walk to the stadium; stand in line to get in; then face another line at the concession stands. But once he/she walks out into the grandstand area, sees the green expanse of the outfield, the infield dirt, the white foul lines and those guys in uniform tossing the ball around there is a sense of peace. Yes, baseball fan, you've arrived. It's time to play ball. As Ernie Banks says, "might as well play two."

Once on a trip to California I was privileged to visit the Crystal Cathedral where Dr. Robert Schuller preached an uplifting message each Sunday. Everything about that church is positive and inspiring from its glass architecture to its friendliness and excitement in calling on a variety of talents to worship and praise the Lord.

Dr. Schuller was the Ernie Banks of ministers. He always had a smile on his face and was always positive and upbeat. Just as Banks loved playing baseball, Schuller loved preaching God's word.

Each service at the Crystal Cathedral began with the singing of the song, "This is the Day the Lord Hath Made." This short song is taken directly from Psalm 118:24 which says: "This is the day the Lord hath made. Let us be glad and rejoice in it." That is wonderful advice. Yet some days we don't think about doing that.

We might be in a bad mood. Something may have happened to anger, disappoint or depress us. Rejoicing is the farthest thing from our current thinking. The NLT Bible (pg. 949) says, "When you don't feel like rejoicing, tell God how you truly feel. You will find that God will give you a reason to rejoice. God has given you this day to live and to serve him—be glad!"

When you think about it just waking up and being privileged to enjoy the new day God has created—a day unlike any before it in history— is cause for rejoicing. When we greet each day as a special gift from our Heavenly Father, give thanks for it and rejoice that we can enjoy another splendid day, then we can say. "Thank you, Lord. It is a great day. Let's play two."

Big Inning Baseball Quote #78:

You gotta love his enthusiasm:

"It's a great day for a ball game. Let's play two."

---Ernie Banks---

Diamond Lesson #79

Take Me Out to the Ball Game

…I will utter hidden things, things from of old. What we have heard and known, what our fathers have told us.   Psalm 78: 2-3

One day Jack Norworth, a Ziegfield Follies performer and co-writer of a number of Tin Pan Alley hit songs, was riding on a subway in New York City when he spied a sign that read: "Ballgame today at the Polo Grounds." It inspired him to write a song about baseball. The one he wrote would be even bigger than any one of his other mega-hits, "Shine on Harvest Moon." In fact, the ditty he penned that day is considered to be one of the most widely sung songs in America. Chances are at any baseball game you've attended you've heard the Norworth creation: "Take Me Out to the Ballgame."

It is sung in the traditional seventh inning stretch. Few fans would recognize the first verse of the song Norworth wrote:

> "Nelly Kelly loved baseball games
> Knew the players, knew all their names,
> You could see her there everyday,
> Shout "Hurray" when they'd play
> Her boy friend by the name of Joe
> Said, "To Coney isle, dear, let's go,"
> Then Nelly started to fret and pout,
> And to him I heard her shout."

Now here comes the part we all know: THE CHORUS

> "Take me out to the ball game,
>   Take me out with the crowd
>   Buy me some peanuts and Cracker Jack,
>   I don't care if I never get back,
>   Let me root, root, root for the home team,
>   If they don't win it's a shame.
>   For it's one, two, three strikes, you're out,
>   At the old ball game."

The Psalmist in Psalm 78 is talking about word of mouth traditions from the fathers passed down through the ages to those listening in the present. Just like "Take Me out to the Ballgame" these stories and songs had survived the ages.

He is speaking in a parable, the kind of teaching style that Jesus would often use later. According to *Nelson's Bible Dictionary (pg. 943)* a parable is "a short, simple story designed to communicate a spiritual truth, religious principal, or a moral lesson; a figure of speech in which truth is illustrated by a comparison or example drawn from everyday experiences."

People knew what a parable was. When the Psalmist said, " I will open my mouth in parables," (NIV) they knew a story was coming and they paid attention. They knew that it would not only be an interesting story from the past, but it would be one with modern applications. People listen if a story has immediate relevance to their own lives.

The fact that he was going to tell, "hidden things of old" meant that this wouldn't be a rehash of some worn out old, cliché-ridden tale they had heard many times before. He would be calling on some of the stories they knew, but this was going to be new, old stuff. It would not only reveal something they didn't know from those old stories, but it would be relevant to their lives that very day.

History provides a mirror to the future. Even though times change, we can learn from the past. This was what the Psalmist was saying. If the people could understand how God had dealt with their ancestors, they could get a grasp on how he would direct, provide for, and love them. It was the same song, but a different verse and it had survived to the present time just as a simple song like "Take Me out to the Ballgame" has.

Big Inning Baseball Quote #79:

So that's why this announcer continued the tradition:

"I would always sing, "Take Me Out to the Ballgame" because I think it is the only song I knew the words to."

---Harry Caray---
famous baseball play-byplay guy

Diamond Lesson #80

Playoffs Mean You Ain't There Yet

So, I have come down to rescue them from the hand of the Egyptians and to bring them out of that land into a good and spacious land, a land flowing with milk and honey.   Exodus 3:8

Remember the days when the American League had eight teams and the National League a like number? Each league had one pennant winner and they met in the World Series; no playoffs (unless two teams tied for the top spot). Simple. Uncomplicated. Boring. Well, it wasn't exactly boring, but it shortened the season and accelerated the excitement.

In 1969 after the two leagues had expanded to 12 teams each, which was divided into two divisions, the first playoffs ensued. Baltimore beat Minnesota by taking three straight games and won the right to play the New York Mets in the World Series. The Mets had swept Atlanta in three games. The Mets went on to win the World Series.

By 1995 the leagues had expanded to 28 teams. Each league had three divisions and now a divisional playoff was added. The winners of the divisional playoff then played for the pennant in the League Championship series. Then those winners met in the World Series. In the end, the Braves defeated the Indians for their first World Championship since 1957.

Currently with 30 teams total and three divisions in each league, they have added two wild cards to the playoffs with the three division winners in each league. The wild card teams play one game to see who joins the three division winners to play their way to the World Series competition between the two leagues.

262

The College Baseball playoff system now resembles that of the Major Leagues. In 1999, the NCAA added a Super Regional to the playoff mix that is similar to the Major League playoff set up. The winners of the 16 Regionals compete at eight Super Regional sites and those eight winners advance to the College World Series.

The Playoffs add excitement and a chance to achieve the ultimate goal of winning a World Series. But getting to the playoffs simply means "you ain't there yet." There's still work to do.

It could have been said the Israelites reached the playoffs when, led by Moses, they escaped from Egypt. They had been slaves for many years during which thoughts of the Promised Land and a better life had grown dim.

Then Moses came along, and under God's direction, got them out of slavery and on the road to the Promised Land. Moses had promised to lead them to a "good and spacious land, a land flowing with milk and honey" but, they still had work to do. They had to be patient and follow God's directions. Seemed simple, but they didn't do it.

While wandering around the wilderness on the way to the Promised Land, they soon forgot the miraculous rescue God had provided for them. They began to grumble, and complain and whine. They angered God with their shortsightedness so he withheld the Promised Land from all but two of them. Joshua and Caleb, who had stayed positive and believed in God's promise to give them the new land, made it. The rest didn't.

Throwing away the opportunity God had provided for them, the Israelites resembled a team that plays hard and makes the playoffs, then forgets "they ain't there yet." When they slack off they never gain the ultimate reward.

Big Inning Baseball Quote #80:

This player spends so much time in the playoffs he doesn't spend a lot of time at home:

"Shaq's house is in such a great neighborhood the bird feeders have salad bars."

---Pat Williams---
Orlando Magic, NBA on Shaquille O'Neal

(not a baseball quote, but you'll have to admit this is a great one)

Diamond Lesson #81

Scouting

...the Lord seeth not as man seeth, for man looketh on the outward appearance, but the Lord looketh on the heart.   1 Samuel 16:7b

You see them in the stands with their notepads and stopwatches. Sometimes they have a radar gun with them. They are looking for talent. They will go anywhere to find a player—from the grassless sandlots in small towns and inner cities to the glistening new stadiums of major college baseball programs. They are the major league scouts.

Whatever it takes to find future major-leaguers, they'll do. They are always looking for a diamond-in-the-rough and hoping that competing scouts won't find out what they have discovered. A Cox News Service article (8-22-05) revealed when Paul Snyder, the Braves super scout, went to Puerto Rico he hid under the bleachers to watch 15-year old catcher Javy Lopez play, so word wouldn't get out to other talent-hungry scouts.

When a scout looks at a player he analyzes his potential on the basis of five tools: hitting, power hitting, fielding, arm strength, and speed. In the case of a pitcher they are looking at what pitches he can throw, his command of those pitches and his composure.

In the early 2000's a new wrinkle was thrown into the scouting process when Billy Beane arrived on the scene in Oakland. As Michael Lewis points out in *Moneyball,* scouting had always been done by former ballplayers who drove thousands of miles, stayed in crummy motels, and while eating non-nutritious meals watched over 200 high school and college games in four months.

Beane changed that thinking by selecting players from a computer. His assistant had set up in his computer all of the major statistical categories they considered in choosing a player. Every college player in America was in that database. That's where the A's started and often ended their scouting process. The computer did the scouting for them. Radical approach, but who can argue with the results the A's had? No matter how it is done effective scouting is an important ingredient in any team's success.

The leadership of the Israelites had always come from judges. When Samuel grew old the people demanded that a king be appointed to rule and lead them into battle against their enemies. He warned them against having a king who would take all the best of everything for himself. They insisted. So God told Samuel, "Do as they say for it is me they are rejecting, not you. They don't want me to be their king any longer."

So a candidate was found. "...Saul was the most handsome man in Israel—head and shoulders taller than anyone else in the land." (1 Samuel 9:2) Saul ruled as king, but eventually became consumed by his own power and disobeyed God. When he was confronted with his sin he rationalized but Samuel wouldn't listen. As he walked away Saul grabbed and tore his cloak. Then Samuel said: "The Lord has torn the kingdom from your hands today and given it to someone else." (1 Samuel 15:28)

The people's choice had failed, so God sent Samuel to anoint His choice. Far from having the dominating appearance of Saul, the new king-to-be was much different. He was a lowly shepherd boy named David. What was different was that he was God's choice. For God looked in the heart, not on the outer appearance. Within, God saw the talent that lay there. He had scouted out the right player to be king.

Big Inning Baseball Quote #81:

Sometimes a scout just gets lucky:

"I did not go out there to look at Gehrig. I did not even know what position he played. But, he played in the outfield against Rutgers and socked a couple of balls a mile. I sat up and took notice. I saw a tremendous youth with powerful arms and terrific legs. I said, 'Here is a kid who can't miss.' "

---Paul Kritchell---
NY Yankees scout

Diamond Lesson #82

Slider

"The serpent tricked me," Eve replied.   Genesis 3:13

"The rotational inertia of an object (baseball) is directly related to its rate of rotation." Huh? Sounds like something Yogi would say if he knew big words like that. Well, let me put it this way. "Objects with large rotational inertia (slider) require a large force to overcome it, while objects with small rotational inertia (fastball) require a small force." Clearer now? Maybe not.

Anyway my thanks to Bobby Chandler, pitcher for the Chillicothe Paints, graduate of Cal State University Stanislaus, and future Science teacher. On the website www.csustan.edu Chandler explains, in scientific terms, what makes pitches work.

In everyday fan talk, the three things that cause a baseball to have speed and movement are: 1) Force 2) Friction and 3) Rotation. The strategy selected by the pitcher on each pitch is all about keeping the hitter off balance, so he won't get a good swing. If the pitcher can make him think a certain pitch is coming and throw him a different one he can usually achieve his goal.

One of the trickiest of pitches is the slider. The slider breaks from right to left in a sweeping motion for right-handed pitchers and the opposite for lefties. It's basically what we used to call a curveball when I was striking out batters in American Legion ballgames. Way back then another popular pitch was the drop ball, which broke downward. Nowadays, they call that a curveball.

268

It's important, in throwing a slider, to snap your wrist in a "side to side motion as you release the baseball." Chandler explains, "The science behind the pitch is that the force applied to the index and middle fingers causes the ball to slide when it is thrown."

Oh yeah, one other thing. You don't want the ball to slide over the heart of the plate or it just might slide right out of the park after the batter hits it.

One of the biggest tricks played in the Bible was when the serpent, in Eve's words, tricked her into eating the forbidden fruit. How often does that happen in our lives. No, not eating forbidden fruit, but doing something wrong and then blaming it on somebody else. "Well, I was only following his advice or her suggestion." It's a cop out. A refusal to take responsibility or blame for a wrong action.

Someone can give us bad advice, but we don't have to believe it, accept it, or act on it. It is all up to us. Of course, some things may be so deceptive that we are fooled into believing them. Still, we have to take responsibility for our actions. It is up to us to do our own "due diligence."

Okay, so I realize that Eve couldn't go on the internet and check out the serpent's credentials. What it came down to with her was a choice. Who do you believe, Eve, God or the Serpent? If her desire to taste that great looking fruit had not overpowered her common sense, she would have realized that the serpent's logic was faulty. She had been given instructions by her Creator and she chose to disobey them. Bye, Bye, Garden of Eden. Hello, world of work, sin and struggles. When the serpent threw the tricky pitch, Eve didn't go to God for advice. It's the same kind of trick pitch Satan still throws and why we must consult God on the decisions we make. He'll help us know if it's a tricky slider or a fat pitch.

Big Inning Baseball Quote #82:

When the batter hits your slider, it's good to have help from a friend:

"My best pitch is anything the batter grounds, lines, or pops in the direction of Phil Rizzuto.

---Vic Raschi---
Yankees Pitcher

Diamond Lesson #83

Go on Contact

I know all the things you do, that you are neither hot nor cold.   Revelation 3:15

Maybe I'm old fashioned, but there's one strategy that seems a lot more prominent in baseball than when I was growing up. It is called "go on contact." As a youngster, the few times I got on third base I was always told, don't run until you see the ball go through the infield. In my years of broadcasting games I was always opposed to the "go on contact" strategy, until FSU's assistant coach Mike Martin Jr. explained it to me.

Mike Jr. said that probably 80% of the college coaches use this strategy, but you have to do it at the right time. "If there is one out and runners are on first and third that's when you want to force the action at the plate." As soon as the ball is hit the runner takes off for home. You don't necessarily have to have a speedster at third base to make this work either. "If you have average speed at third and he takes off on contact and that throw is just a little off line, he'll beat it," Martin added.

When not to do it Mike Jr. says, "If there is nobody out and I'm at third, I'm staying, You don't want to make the first out at the plate or kill a potential rally.

There are other times when you don't want to do it. "If you have a Shane Robinson up and say, and Aaron Cheeseman is on third you won't do it," Martin said. The reasoning being Robinson, College Baseball's Player of the Year with a .427 batting average, wass likely to deliver an RBI hit. Also, Cheeseman, like most catchers, did not have great speed. So if Robinson hit the ball hard, which he did a lot, and it happened to go to a fielder with the infield drawn in, Cheese would be a sitting duck at the plate.

Martin Jr. points out that in a blowout game you wouldn't use this strategy. Don't want to risk an injury at the plate when the game is practically decided.

Asked for an example of "going on contact" working well in a key situation Coach Martin Jr. told this story: In 2005, playing Auburn, with a runner at third, RF Jack Rye took a mighty swing and barely topped the ball. "I bet that ball didn't even reach the grass in front of home," Mike said. Catching everyone off-balance the "going on contact" run scored easily. Making up your mind to go as soon as the ball is hit is the key. Hesitation, uncertainty, or a late start won't work.

In *Revelation* John records letters from the Lord to different churches explaining where they fall short of the requirements in the Kingdom. The Church at Laodicea is warned that they have a big problem. They are neither hot nor cold, but lukewarm. They are a bunch of fence sitters. They won't declare what they believe, get off the fence, and back up their beliefs. That's the worst kind. Like a drink that is lukewarm; it is spit out. Some drinks are meant to be hot, some cold, but none taste better in a lukewarm state.

John says it would be better to be spiritually cold, than lukewarm. (QSB, pg. 1714.) "At least those who are spiritually cold cannot pretend that they are all right. Their spiritual needs are obvious. But those who are lukewarm may have just enough pretense of religion to cause them to think they are okay. God desires wholehearted, sincere responses. Anything less suggests that other things have a higher priority than a relationship with Him. Those who want "the minimum requirement," just enough of God to get by—risk missing Him altogether." To succeed in "going on contact" in baseball your mind must be made up, then act strongly. God's requirements are the same.

272

Big Inning Baseball Quote #83:

A player who was often in position to go on contact:

"Nellie Fox, that little son-of-a-gun was always on base and was a great hit-and-run man.

He sprayed hits all over."

---Yogi Berra---
NY Sunday News, July 12, 1970

Diamond Lesson #84

Tommy John Surgery

Have compassion on me, Lord, for I am weak. Heal me, Lord, for my body is in agony. I am sick at heart. How long, O Lord, until you restore me?   Psalm 6:2-3

Ulnar collateral ligament reconstruction (UCL) is a surgical procedure commonly known as Tommy John surgery. It was first performed on the Dodger lefty, by famous sports surgeon Dr. Frank Jobe, when John was 31. After a year and a half of rehab John returned to action and pitched in the Majors until he was 46.

This radical surgical procedure consists of replacing a ligament in the elbow with a tendon from another area such as the patient's forearm, hamstring, or foot. When John had his surgery Dr. Jobe gave him 1 in 100 chances to be able to pitch again. Nowadays, the estimated recovery rate is set at 85 to 90%. In fact, it is not uncommon for a pitcher to throw even harder after recovery from this surgery than he threw before his injury. The reason being the rigorous rehabilitation procedure he has to undergo.

Mike Dodd in a 2003 USA Today article said that doctors usually complete the surgery in about an hour. That's about a third of the time it took Jobe to repair Tommy John in the original one. Usually the patient doesn't even have to stay in the hospital overnight.

Reliever Billy Koch, who blew out his elbow in his third professional appearance in 1997 came back to register 163 saves between 1999 and 2004 and often hit 100 mph with his fastball. Koch said with a smile, "It felt so good when I came back I said I recommend it to everyone, regardless what your ligament looks like."

A few of the Major League pitchers who have survived Tommy John Surgery include: John Smoltz, Mariano Rivera, Kris Benson, A. J. Burnett, Paul Byrd, Ryan Dempster, Tom Gordon, Mike Hampton, Jason Isringhausen, Kerry Wood, and Bob Wickman.

No longer do pitchers with a "dead arm," the old-time description of ligament damage, have to end their careers. Tommy John surgery puts them back on track.

Just as God oversees Tommy John surgery he is watching over our physical well-being everyday. The God who watches over and protects a universe that could be blown away by a nuclear blast, is also in control of every person's physical well-being.

King David knew that. He prayed in earnest for God's mercy and for his healing. In his times of sorrow David became so distraught that he was physically sick. We read of such a time in Psalm 6. With a little bit of exaggeration David says he is so distraught that he has cried all night and his tears are so plentiful they have drenched his couch.

The QSB Bible (pg. 733) points out "David's severe sorrow caused faintness, agony, anguish, groaning and weeping. He was speaking with poetic flair, probably exaggerating his emotional state."

The *Believer's Bible Commentary (pg. 554)* points out the dire straits that David found himself in saying he was suffering double trouble. He had a serious illness that was compounded by the pressure of his opponents. David thought the sickness was a stroke of God brought on by some sin. It is true that God sometimes permits illness as a way of displaying his power and glory. But, all healing, no matter if it is miraculous like Tommy John surgery or ordinary comes from the Lord. David understood this and prayed and received healing from God.

Big Inning Baseball Quote #84:

The need for Tommy John Surgery makes a pitcher nervous, this one didn't even need surgery to induce nervousness:

"Lew would make coffee nervous."

---Fred Haney---
Braves Manager on Lew Burdette

Diamond Lesson #85

Rain Delay

When Noah was 600 years old, on the 17th day of the second month, the underground waters burst forth on earth, and the rain fell in mighty torrents from the sky. The rain continued to fall for forty days and forty nights.   Genesis 7:11-12

The two most dreaded words in baseball after, "You're Out," are "Rain Delay." "Oh no, here am I stuck at the ball park with no action going on and my umbrella is in my car." Of course, even if you had your umbrella you wouldn't leave the stadium until you see if the game is called. If they resume play, you dry off your seat, and settle down to watch the rest of the game.

The rules say it is up to the home team to decide if a game will start when it is raining. Once the game is underway the umpires take control of every aspect of it. This includes whether or not to invoke a rain delay or if they should call the game. They also decide if playing field conditions warrant continuing to play.

In college baseball the NCAA has instituted a new rule that governs playing the game with lightning in the area. The rule says if a lighting strike has been spotted in the area (within eight miles of the ball park) play will be suspended for a minimum of 30 minutes or until the lightning ceases. Even though it may not be raining, the game may be stopped.

On opening day 2006 a beeper went off at Dick Howser Stadium where Florida State was playing Charleston Southern. Randy Oravetz the Seminoles head trainer pointed out that wasn't an ordinary beeper. It was connected to Weather Data in Wichita, Kansas, a company that monitors the USA for potential lightning strikes. They give an advisory when lightning is 15 miles away. Randy said if it reaches 8 miles away everybody vacates the field. Then the game doesn't start back for at least 30 minutes. In the meantime they check local radar and also Vaisala, a service in Arizona, that shows actual lightning strikes in all areas on the computer screen. Twice in that FSU game the beeper went off meaning delays totaling an hour, after which the game was called. Rain delays are not fun, but lightning delays are even worse.

One time God caused a big rain delay on earth. This one lasted 40 days and nights. Genesis 6:5 says: "The Lord saw how great man's wickedness on the earth had become and that every inclination of the thoughts of his heart was only evil all the time." God got fed up. No matter how many opportunities or how much slack God cut mankind, the people refused to change their ways, so God decided to destroy the whole shooting match. He would flood the earth and wipe out every living thing.

God noticed that Noah was a righteous man. Rewarding his lifestyle, God told Noah what was going to happen. He instructed Noah to "make an ark of Cypress wood." and provided Noah specific instructions on building it. It would be 450 feet long, 75 feet wide, and 45 feet high. It was strong enough to withstand the floodwaters and big enough to hold "two of all living creatures male and female, to keep them alive." (Gen. 6:19)

Noah obeyed God and the biggest of all rain delays began. (Gen 7:22) "Every living thing on the face of the earth was wiped out." But Noah, the righteous man was spared, along with his family and all the animals that were in the ark. Then God established a covenant with Noah promising that he would never destroy the earth by flooding again. Thank goodness! Still, this rain delay story points out the importance of living a life that is pleasing to God.

Big Inning Baseball Quote #85:

And this is true whether it is raining or not:

"If people don't want to come to the ballpark, how are you gonna stop them?"

---Yogi Berra---

Diamond Lesson #86

Knuckler

The fastest runner doesn't always win the race and the strongest warrior doesn't always win the battle.   Ecclesiastes 9:11

The knuckleball. Everyman's pitch! "An almost mythic pitch that reduces great hitters to making cartoonish swings at the ball," says Ben McGrath in an interview with *The New Yorker Magazine* colleague Lauren Porcaro. In praise of the knuckler McGrath adds why he likes the pitch "it holds out the idea that there is not some kind of impossible separation between the fan and the all-star-that with the proper amount of guile and cunning, you or I could strike out Barry Bonds, (O. K., maybe not Bonds, but possibly Jason Giambi.)"

From the stands the knuckleball looks like it is so slow that anybody could throw it. Conversely, it looks like anybody should be able to hit this off speed pitch when compared to one of those 100 mph fastballs. But it ain't that easy. Whereas breaking pitches and fastballs rely a lot on force and the spin on the ball, the knuckler is the opposite. The knuckle ball pitcher tries to take all the spin off the pitch. Then, the airflow over the seams creates an erratic and unpredictable movement. Consequently the batter may be swinging in one area while the baseball is moving into another one.

One of the reasons the batters have such a tough time hitting a knuckler is that the pitcher has trouble controlling it. He usually doesn't even know where it's going to end up. You can pity the poor catcher who has to try to catch the knuckler and the umpire who is trying to watch closely and determine if it went over the plate or not. If the knuckle ball doesn't get any movement, watch out. That ball could be hit a long way.

280

It seems those hard throwers win the most games, but that is not always the case. Hoyt Wilhelm, Phil Niekro and Tim Wakefield, three prominent knuckleball pitchers, had won 605 games (through 2005).

At the end of his life King Solomon, reputed to be the world's wisest man came to the conclusion that the fastest runner doesn't always win the race and the strongest warrior doesn't always win the battle. Solomon had observed a lot of situations before he made this observation. In everyday life we see underdogs often win. Solomon said "It is all determined by chance and being in the right place at the right time. People can never predict when hard times might come. Like fish in a net or birds in a snare, people are often caught by sudden tragedy." (Ecclesiastes 9:11-12) We know from experience and from scripture that hard work dedicated to God is a prescription for victory. Colossians 3:23 says, "Work hard and cheerfully at whatever you do, as though you were working for the Lord rather than for people."

Even though Solomon seems to be trying to reduce our expectations in his observations by saying that luck plays a role that might even be greater than a person who is best at something could overcome. QSB (pg. 922) says, "So often it seems that we have no control over the events of our lives, that blind chance determines who succeeds…The Bible as a whole, however, teaches the opposite. God is concerned about everyone and deals with people fairly. What we don't see is that accounts are not all settled in this lifetime." Sometimes a slower knuckler wins out over a more powerful fastball.

Big Inning Baseball Quote #86:

A catcher who has it figured out:

"The best way to catch a knuckleball is to wait until it stops rolling and pick it up."

---Bob Uecker---
Former catcher, broadcaster

Diamond Lesson #87

Rhubarb

Don't have anything to do with foolish, stupid arguments because you know they produce quarrels.   2 Timothy 2:23

Red Barber, the legendary play-by-play guy for the Dodgers called his autobiography, "Rhubarb in the Catbird Seat." Red had often referred to Ebbets Field, where he broadcast the home games, as the "rhubarb patch." The reason being that "Dem Bums," as the Brooklyn team was referred to, often got into a lot of arguments with the umpires.

The New Dickson Baseball Dictionary defines rhubarb as "a ruckus with the umpire(s) or a fight between players or between the players and fans." It dates the first use of the term to 1943 and attributes it to the old Redhead (Barber), who it says "got it from either Brooklyn-born sportswriter Garry Schumacher or from Tom Meany, another sportswriter, who said he had picked it up in a bar in Brooklyn in the late 1930's."

Actually rhubarb is a plant that can be grown year around in warm climates. It has a tart taste and is often used in stews. But, Rhubarb Pie, is also popular. Of course, you might want to add a little sugar (about ½ to ¾ cup should work) to the pie recipe to sweeten it up. Rhubarb can certainly stir up the taste buds, just like a baseball rhubarb adds a different element to the game.

Anything to do with a rhubarb is something out of the ordinary. Take the 1951 movie *Rhubarb* starring Ray Milland, Jan Sterling and Gene Lockhart. The plot revolves around a crusty old millionaire T. J. Banner (Lockhart) who dies and leaves all his money and his baseball team, the Brooklyn Loons, to his cat named…you guessed it…Rhubarb.

It was bad enough that the Loons were the laughing stock of baseball for having a cat as a mascot, but now Rhubarb, with team publicist Eric Yaeger (Milland) as protector, owns the team. Yaeger convinces the team that Rhubarb is good luck and the Loons begin to win. They've gone from a bunch of losers to winners, thanks to a little Rhubarb.

Christians are advised in 2 Timothy not to get involved in rhubarbs. We can't effectively present God's truth in an argumentative state. Paul told Timothy to be "kind and gentle, patiently and courteously explaining the truth." (NLT). We are supposed to listen attentively to questions and treat others opinions with respect, so we may make our points in an acceptable manner.

Quarreling gets us nowhere. It destroys opportunities for making rational decisions. Paul advised Titus (Titus 3:9-QSB) to defend the essentials of his beliefs that are central to our salvation: faith, repentance and submission to the will of God. He said to "avoid foolish controversies and genealogies and arguments about the law because they are unprofitable and useless." Defending core beliefs is important. Doing it in an argumentative manner is improper.

The Message (pg. 2171) puts it this way: "God's servant must not be argument-ative, but a gentle listener and a teacher who keeps cool, working firmly but patiently with those who refuse to obey." When this kind of an approach is adopted the person you want to receive the information God has put on your heart is more likely to be receptive.

The last thing you want to do is get involved in a rhubarb!

Big Inning Baseball Quote #87:

In addition to putting up with rhubarbs:

"An umpire is expected to be perfect the day you start and then improve."

---Ed Vargo---
Umpire

Diamond Lesson #88

Fighting All Night

So, Jacob was left alone and a man wrestled with him until daybreak.   ***Genesis 32:24***

There are some games that you know will be a fight to the finish. Both teams will fight all night to win the game. You can't count them out no matter how far behind either team falls. These are the games that Yogi was thinking about when he uttered his famous saying: "It ain't over 'til it's over."

On June 18, 1911, the Detroit Tigers trailed the Chicago Whitesox by 12 runs after five and a half innings. Led by Ty Cobb, the Tigers came roaring back to win 16-15. They never stopped fighting or believed the game was over.

On June 15, 1925 Connie Mack's Philadelphia Athletics trailed the Cleveland Indians 15-4 after seven and a half innings. But the A's scored 13 runs in the bottom of the 8th to pull out a 17-15 victory. The Mackmen just kept on fighting.

The third game in major league history in which a team trailed by as many as 12 runs and came back to win would not come until August 5, 2001, at Jacobs Field, Cleveland, Ohio. By the bottom of the 6th inning the Seattle Mariners had a 14-2 lead and Manager Lou Pinella decided to give some starters a little rest. Ichiro Suzuki, Edgar Martinez, and John Olerud went to the bench. Cleveland had already pulled most of their starters. With Roberto Alomar, Ellis Burks, Travis Fryman, and Juan Gonzalez benched and down by 12 they looked dead in the water. Many fans thought so and headed for the exit. What they didn't realize was that these Indians would fight all night. A Jim Thome homer, his second of the night and league leading 36th, helped the Tribe pull to within six,

14-9, in the 8th. With two outs in the bottom of the ninth the Indians still trailed by five runs. The Mariners could not nail down the final out. Remember "it ain't over 'til it's over." With the bases loaded, Omar Vizquel ripped a triple to the right field corner to tie the game 14-14.

Now the Indians had momentum. Their 20,000 remaining fans were into it. After four hours and eleven minutes, Jolbert Cabrera hit a broken bat single scoring the fleet Kenny Lofton from second. The Indians had won 15-14 because they fought all night.

In Genesis 32 we read about another Jacob, out in the field, who fought all night. Here's the story. Jacob had cheated his brother Esau out of his birthright by deceiving their father, Isaac, who was in ill health with failing eyesight.

To avoid Esau's rage, Jacob fled to Paddan Aram where he went to work for Laban and eventually married both of his daughters Leah and Rachel. Laban deceived him into first marrying Leah. Then Jacob eventually married Rachel, the one he really loved. Now he was set to return home and face Esau. He dreaded that part.

On the trip, as they camped out in the fields, Jacob sent his family ahead across a brook to safety and stayed behind. There he spent the night, met and wrestled with a man who some commentaries called an angel of the Lord. The two fought all night and near daybreak Jacob still would not let go even after his hip was dislocated. He told the man he would not release him until he received the Lord's blessing. By fighting all night Jacob was blessed by the Lord and his name was changed to Israel. Thus, he became the father of the 12 tribes of Israel.

Big Inning Baseball Quote #88:

Talk about a fighter, here's one:

"If I were playing third base and my mother were rounding third with the run that was going to beat us, I'd trip her.   Oh I'd pick her up and brush her off and say, 'Sorry Mom,' but nobody beats me."

--Leo Durocher---

Diamond Lesson #89

McGillicuddy

And Daniel could understand visions and dreams of all kinds.   Daniel 1:17

Cornelius McGillicuddy was his real name and he managed in the Major Leagues for 53 years while wearing a coat and tie. His baseball name was Connie Mack and he is best known for managing and owning the Philadelphia Athletics for 50 years. Just what kind of a man stays in the same job for one-half of a century?

Arthur Daley captured the essence of the man they called "The Tall Tactician" in a 1949 *New York Times* article. Always a pleasant and soft-spoken man, Mack was approached by a stranger in a hotel lobby one day when he was 86 years old. The enthusiastic stranger said that he had always wanted to shake his hand and added, "I've followed your career in baseball for more than 50 years, Mr. Griffith."

"Thank you, thank you," chirped baseball's oldest inhabitant in his gentle voice, smiling with that shy smile of his, "but I'm not Clark Griffith, I'm Connie Mack."

The man said, "But, you look like Clark Griffith."

Not wanting to embarrass the main Mack replied, "You're perfectly right, we look almost alike except for the fact that I am 6-foot-2 and Grif is 5-foot-2. I'm built like a rail and he's well, by golly, I guess I have to say he is slightly better built. But, I can easily understand how we could be mistaken for each other any place."

In addition to being the world's nicest person, Mr. McGillicuddy was a pretty fair manager. He holds the record for managing the most games with a total of 7,878. Mack also has the record for wins with 3,776.

As The Sports Devotional Bible (pg. 1002) points out that 53 years managing and 50 of those in the same city is amazing, yet a person in the Bible topped that. "While that seems like a long time to live in one city doing one task, it falls about 17 years short of the length of time Daniel resided in the capital of Babylon as God's representative."

TSDB adds, "For 70 years, from 605 to 536 B. C., Daniel managed to prosper in enemy territory. Indeed, he flourished there and had the presence of mind to record the events for our reading. Daniel is one of the most intriguing, faithful characters in God's Word. From the beginning of his time in Babylon to the end of it, he trusted God implicitly and obeyed him openly. Few Bible characters share the flawless record Daniel enjoyed as he lived for God throughout his life."

Daniel is such a good example for us to follow because his life was one of total obedience to God despite the circumstances. Daniel and three of his friends were taken as teenagers from their home in Judah to Babylonia. Because of his faithfulness, God enabled Daniel to find favor with the king by interpreting his dreams. This made the other administrators and princes jealous and they sought a way to trip up Daniel through his religion. They convinced the king to make a decree that anyone who prayed to any divine or human being besides the king for thirty days would be thrown to the lions.

Naturally when this decree went out Daniel continued to pray to God and didn't try to hide it. He was thrown in the lion's den where he stayed overnight. When the king went to the den the next morning he found Daniel completely unharmed. Then king Darius said, "I decree that everyone throughout my kingdom should tremble with fear before the God of Daniel." (Daniel 7:26) So Daniel, like Connie Mack, did the right thing and was granted much success in Babylon for a long time.

Big Inning Baseball Quote #89:

Talk about being around for a long time:

"I just know it's an ugly rumor that you and I are the only two people alive who saw

Abner Doubleday throw the first pitch.

---Ronald Reagan—
talking to 300 game winner Gaylord Perry

Diamond Lesson #90

The Art of Bunting

This should be your ambition; to live a quiet life minding your own business.
                                                                    1 Thessalonians 4:11

In his book *Bunts* George Will writes, "Bunts are modest and often useful things, although they are not always well understood, even by those who are supposed to know when and how to lay them down." In fact, it is not even clear how the term bunt originated but one popular theory is that the term is derived from "buntling" which designates a baby hit.

A bunt is basically a batted ball on which a hitter does not take a full swing and simply taps the ball out in front of the plate. There are different kinds of bunts and this strategy is used for different reasons. Mike Martin, who has won over 1,800 games at FSU, distinguishes among the different bunting strategies. "A sacrifice bunt can definitely win ball games," said the Seminoles #11. He frequently calls on a batter to give himself up by bunting a runner into scoring position or from second to third.

Or a hitter can bunt for a base hit. Martin contends that by bunting frequently for a hit a batter can "add 20 to 30 points to his batting average." The key here is that sometimes he will beat it out for a hit. Next time the first and third basemen will play "in" for him, which will enable him to slap a ball past them for a hit. Skilled hitters use drag bunts, where the batter starts in motion as the pitch is on its way bunting on the run.

With a man on third base a coach or manager could employ a squeeze bunt, either a "safety squeeze" or a "suicide squeeze." Martin says, "The safety squeeze is an easy way to score a run if the infield is playing back. That way you don't run the risk of a

292

routine popup or strikeout ruining a scoring opportunity." It catches the defense off guard. On the other hand, on a suicide squeeze the runner starts for home as the pitcher starts his motion. The batter must put the ball in play or the runner will be tagged out. It is a bold, exciting, and somewhat risky strategy. By properly mixing the various kinds of bunts into their offensive strategies a team can pick up a lot of extra victories.

As Coach Martin points out, a successful bunt attempt doesn't get as much attention as an unsuccessful one does, but bunts are important. Executing a bunt sets an example of being a team player. In Thessalonians Paul calls on the church members to be team players by being "a model to all believers."

Paul goes on to say in 1 Thessalonians 4:11 that they can do this by setting as a goal that of leading a quiet life, not one of showboating or trying to draw attention to ourselves in the extreme. We have to be responsible in all areas of our lives.

Paul admonished those who were looking for handouts that they should set an example by working hard. That is what others will respect. This would enable them to share their faith and to have an impact on others. Nobody likes a slacker. There is no honor in holding back and letting others do all the work, while you share the benefits. That's like a player who wants to be exempt from laying down a bunt and always wants the green light to swing away. He thinks more of his own stats than the team's welfare.

The Believer's Bible Commentary enlarges on Paul's instructions saying that he encouraged the saints to do three things: a) Don't seek after the limelight, but be "little and unknown, loved and prized by Christ alone; b) Mind your own business instead of butting into other people's affairs; c) Be self-supporting. Don't be a parasite or a moocher, sponging off others. Christians are called on to bunt for others welfare.

293

Big Inning Baseball Quote #90:

This usually didn't happen even in a pitcher's dreams:

"When Mickey Mantle bunted with the wind blowing out in Crosley Field."

                    ---Robin Roberts---
                on his greatest All Star thrill

Diamond Lesson #91

Diamond Talk

Then, what looked like tongues of fire appeared and settled on each of them. And everyone present was filled with the Holy Spirit and began speaking in other languages as the Holy Spirit gave them this ability. ***Acts 2:3-4***

The one and only Yogi Berra once said of the diamond game, "It ain't like football. You can't make up no trick plays." Baseball is in fact unlike any other game. That's why it has its own special language. For example a pitcher who got "raked" is not one who was standing on the mound when the groundskeepers were preparing it for the game. He is raked when he gives up lots of runs and hits in an appearance. That's about the same as getting "roughed up."

"In a slump" can refer to a team who hasn't won many games lately or a player who hasn't been able to get a base hit.

Sweeping the bases doesn't mean a player gets out a broom and starts a dust storm around the infield. It means he knocks in all the runners on base as with a bases loaded double or triple. He could also be credited with "clearing the bases" or "cleaning the bases." Could even be a "standup triple" meaning the batter gets there ahead of the ball and doesn't have to slide.

A "keystone hit" is not one made by the Keystone Kops, but one that enables the batter to reach second base. Could also be a double or a two-bagger or what they call an "Aparicio double" named after the former Whitesox shortstop who got lots of walks that he followed with a stolen base.

"Tweeners" are balls hit between the outfielders as are "gap shots." "Scrubs" are players who are available to substitute for starting players and they are members of the "bench bunch." Yes, baseball has a language of it's own, one that cannot be applied to other sports.

Not everyone speaks the same language and in the Book of Acts, Luke wrote of the day in which God dramatically spoke to a multitude of people, each in their own language. It was "the day of Pentecost, seven weeks after Jesus' resurrection and the believers were meeting together in one place." Since Pentecost was one of three major festivals there was a large international audience present.

Then God got their attention with a sound from heaven like the roaring of a mighty windstorm. This was followed by flames or tongues of fire that settled on each of them. Then a very remarkable thing happened. "And everyone present was filled with the Holy Spirit and began speaking in other languages, as the Holy Spirit gave them this ability." (Acts 2:4)

The Jews were amazed because here were people from all different places, but they could hear them speaking in a language they could understand. The only thing they could think of was that these people were drunk. That was unlikely; it was only nine a.m.

Peter pointed out that what was happening had been predicted many years ago by the prophet Joel. "Your old men will dream dreams. Young men will see visions. In those days, I will pour out my spirit even on servants, men and women alike." (Joel 2:28-29). Each person was now sharing one language as God communicated with them.

Big Inning Baseball Quote #91:

The fans have diamond talk of their own:

"I never could play in New York. The first time I ever came into a game there, I got in the bullpen car and they told me to lock the doors."

--Mike Flanagan---
Orioles pitcher

Diamond Lesson #92

Lead by Example

And a voice from heaven said, "This is my Son whom I love; with Him I am well pleased.   Matthew 3:17

Team leaders come in all shapes and sizes from various backgrounds and with unique personalities. One thing that they all have in common is they must lead by example. They can't say one thing and do another. They can't encourage or criticize another for something they can't do or aren't doing themselves. It's the age-old axiom, "if you're going to talk the talk, you must walk the walk."

In the mid-70's Cincinnati's Big Red Machine was the talk of baseball. With a star-studded lineup that included Johnny Bench, Pete Rose, Joe Morgan, George Foster, Ken Griffey (Sr.) and Tony Perez there was plenty of leadership by example. Ask those guys in later years about team leadership and they point to Perez.

Bench, a Hall of Fame inductee like Perez, called Tony the "heart and soul of the Big Red Machine." Bench said Perez wasn't just a player who drove in runs he was a player who drove in THE run, when you needed it.

His manager Sparky Anderson called Perez the best hitter he ever saw when the game was on the line and added, "Tony taught us all the meaning of heart."

Perhaps the greatest example of leading by example was that of Jackie Robinson, the first player to break the color line in the majors. Robinson's strong work ethic, religious roots, and talents enabled him to endure indignities no man should ever have to endure.

Jackie handled death threats, verbal harassment, and physical abuse in his first year with the Brooklyn Dodgers to win the respect of fans and players alike in leading the Dodgers to the pennant. Typical of this classy guy, Robinson deferred the credit to his wife Rachel saying, she was "strong, loving, gentle and brave, she was never afraid to criticize or comfort." With her support and his talent Jackie Robinson lead by example.

God sent his only Son, Jesus, to earth to lead by example. In the greatest act of love ever recorded the Son of our Heavenly Father was born of a human mother, grew to manhood, worked, taught, and performed miracles in order to show us how to live and rescue us from sin.

After Jesus was baptized by John the Baptist, God's voice from Heaven said, "This is my Son in whom I am well-pleased." Then the satanic attacks began. Nothing was held back from Jesus in the way of temptations as he was tested and tempted for 40 days in the wilderness by Satan.

Jesus showed the proper work ethic as he worked hard with his earthly father, Joseph the carpenter. He kept up his studies, while he worked as well. He went to the synagogue and amazed the scholars with the depth of his knowledge.

His compassion and love led Jesus to work miracles of healing in people's lives. He rewarded faith and trust. He healed the sick, restored eyesight, enabled cripples to walk, and even brought Lazarus back from death.

Jesus taught using parables, which were stories with contemporary applications. Most of all he stressed the importance of loving each other. He showed that love was stronger than hate as he was nailed to a cross to save us from our sins and wrongful living. Jesus is the ultimate proof of the importance of leading by example.

Big Inning Baseball Quote #92:

Obviously a good example can be set by knocking the ball out of the park:

"Gimme good hitting and long hitting and let the rest of them managers get just as smart as they want to be."

> **---Wilbert Robinson---**
> **Dodgers Mgr. 1914-31**

Diamond Lesson #93

Official Scorer

Love keeps no record of wrongs.   *1 Corinthians 13:5b*

"You gotta make that play." That's the simple explanation Joey Ferolito had when someone questioned why he scored a particular play an error instead of a base hit. Ferolito, was the official scorer for the post-season games at Florida State University's Dick Howser Stadium. It was his job to make judgment calls on how various plays should be scored. Prime among those being hit or error, wild pitch or passed ball, and any other tricky call that is not obvious. The way Joey scored it is the way it stood. Someone was going to be happy with the call and someone wasn't.

In professional baseball official scorers are appointed by the league and sit in the press box. They send an official record of the game to the league office. They can change a ruling within 24 hours of the close of the game. Larry Stone, *Baseball Digest* writer, in an article on the art of keeping score, talked about Charlie Scoggins, official scorer for the Redsox for 26 years. Retired infielder Jeremy Remy jokingly claims Scoggins kept him out of the Hall of Fame with decisions that took 1,300 hits away from him and kept him from reaching the 3,000 hits total. As a Major League official scorer Scoggins was paid $125 a game. Stone says these scorers claim, "$1 of that is for scoring and $124 is for aggravation."

A situation that puts the official scorer on the hot seat is calling hit or error when a pitcher has a no-hitter going. Making that judgment call, which determines if the pitcher makes the record books or not, can be a very difficult and stressful decision.

In 1992, FSU's Chris Roberts had not just a no-hitter, but also a perfect game going into the late innings. As the tension and suspense mounted Official Scorer Donna Turner, also the team's Baseball Sports Information Director at the time, was hoping she wouldn't face a controversial decision, but she did. In the 8th inning a ground ball was headed for centerfield when the second baseman backhanded it on the outfield grass, then threw wildly to first. Turner took her time in making the ruling. When a base hit was put on the scoreboard, ending the perfect game, the hometowns boos were loud. But Turner knew she had made the right call. Roberts even agreed.

Record keeping is important in baseball. It isn't always that important in life. Keeping score can ruin a relationship. It is natural to count things. That's how we discern success from failure. It's how we measure growth and productivity. By keeping score we can compare this year's figures with last year. Thus, we learn if our company is growing or if our family is making financial progress.

One thing Paul points out in 1 Corinthians 13, the Bible's preeminent chapter on love, is that it doesn't keep score. It "keeps no record of wrongs." In a loving relationship scorekeeping is not important. It is petty. It's shallow. It is hurtful.

Nobody is perfect. There will be inequities in any relationship. If love has its way nobody is counting nor trying to take advantage of each other. Things happen. Being on the same wavelength with someone you love is important. Understanding what things hurt and avoiding them is key. As Paul says, "Love never gives up, never loses faith, is always hopeful and endures through every circumstance." Oh yeah, it has no official scorer, either.

Big Inning Baseball Quote #93:

He's talking about someone who knows the score:

"My wife, (in the divorce) she takes half of everything I make. I give up six runs and three are charged to her."

---Jose Rijo---
Reds pitcher

Diamond Lesson #94

That's Baseball

But, if we confess our sins to Him, He is faithful and just to forgive us and to cleanse us from every wrong.   1 John 1:9

"A hotdog at the ballgame beats roast beef at the Ritz," said legendary movie star Humphrey Bogart. It's a statement that says a lot about the game of baseball and its uniqueness among all sports. There is an atmosphere at a baseball game unlike any other. It's a social game played at a pace and divided into segments that provide time for fans in the stands and players in the dugout and bullpen to chat.

That is not to say that the action is not intense and exciting. Pitcher Earl Wilson once described it: "A baseball game is simply a nervous breakdown divided into nine innings." What a player does on that baseball diamond determines how well he can provide for his family. It's work. Still as Willie Stargell said, "When they start the game, they don't yell, 'Work Ball.' They say, 'Play Ball.' "

There's a little larceny involved in baseball with bases being stolen. Entertainer/Author Woody Allen once said, "When we'd play softball I'd steal second base, feel guilty and go back (to first)." But stealing in this sense is good. As Tom Clark averred, "I'm convinced that every boy, in his heart, would rather steal second base than an automobile."

Baseball is a game that requires intellect. Jim Bouton said "Baseball players are smarter than football players. How often do you see a baseball team penalized for too many men on the field?" And it is a game of accountability where everyone can discern your mistakes. An unknown author once said. "Things could be worse. Suppose your errors were counted and published every day, like those of a baseball player."

There are some puzzling things about the game as Larry Anderson asked, "Why does everybody stand up and sing "Take me out to the ballgame" when they are already there? In baseball things continually happen that are beyond a player, coach or manager's control." These things are best described by FSU's Mike Martin who simply says, "That's baseball."

As believers when we make a mistake it won't likely be broadcast on radio, shown on television or chronicled in the newspaper. In fact, if we confess and ask forgiveness it will be forgiven and forgotten by God. Then we can move on to the next thing in life. In fact, that is what the Lord wants us to do.

Pastor Joel Osteen, in his mega-best selling book *Your Best Life Now* writes, "Let's be frank; sometimes, because of wrong choices, disobedience, or sin, we miss out on God's 'Plan A.' The good news is God has a 'Plan B,''a "Plan C,' and whatever it takes to get us to His final destination for our lives."

Most likely our mistakes are not going to be publicized and even if they are Osteen says: "If you continue to dwell on those past disappointments, you will block God's blessings in your life today. It's simply not worth it."

We are called on to work hard as members of God's team. That will be our biggest contribution and it may require sacrifices as well as forsaking the spotlight. Or God may want attention drawn to our accomplishments as an example for others. Even if it seems life is not always fair we must remember as Osteen points out in his book: "God wants you to be a winner, not a whiner!" That's Life!

Big Inning Baseball Quote #94:

Leave it to a great actor to put the game in true perspective:

"That's baseball and it's my game. Y' know, you take your worries to the game and you leave them there. You yell like crazy for your guys. It's good for your lungs, gives you a lift, and nobody calls the cops. Pretty girls, as well, lots of em."

Humphrey Bogart

Diamond Lesson #95

The World Series

There's an opportune time to do things, a right time for everything on the earth.
Ecclesiastes 3:1

The celebration was 86 years in the making. On April 11, 2005, the Boston Redsox did it up right in a pre-game ceremony. The BoSox celebrated their first World Series championship since 1919 with the Boston Pops and Boston Sympathy dressed in formal attire and playing in centerfield as the large World Champion banner was unfurled. The banner was so large it covered the entire Green Monster, the 37-foot tall left field wall. Forty-seven championship rings were passed out and then the Redsox went out and defeated the New York Yankees, 8-1.

The curse of the Bambino that long-suffering Redsox fans had heard about every year since 1920, when Babe Ruth was traded to the New York Yankees, was broken. In 1918, the Bosox had won their 5th World Championship without a loss. They wouldn't win another until 2004 when they overcame a three-games-to-none deficit to beat the Yankees four-in-a-row, then took four straight from the St. Louis Cardinals to become the Champions.

Just when baseball fans thought they had seen everything, along came the Chicago Whitesox one year later. They had not been to the World Series in 46 years; hadn't won a Series since 1917. The Whitesox had a different kind of a curse. It could be called the curse of the Blacksox because in 1919 they won the pennant, but were accused of throwing the World Series. Eight of their players, including star outfielder Shoeless Joe Jackson, were kicked out of baseball for good.

The 2005 Whitesox overcame that jinx by leading their division every day of the season. With a team consisting of practically unknown players the Pale Hose swept the defending champion Redsox out of the playoffs in three games. They dumped the Angels by winning four of five and swept the Astros 4-0 in the World Series. Baseball Almanac called it the "Year of Redemption for the Windy City."

Baseball fans can't help wondering if another Chicago team will be the next one to overcome a curse. The Cubs have not been to a World Series since 1945 nor have they won one since 1908.

There is a time for everything. In Ecclesiastes, Solomon points out that God has predetermined your time. He knows when the different stages or seasons of your life will occur. The *Believers Bible Commentary* says "there is a predetermined season for everything and a fixed time for every happening. This means God has programmed every activity into a gigantic computer…It also means that history is filled with cyclical patterns, and these recur with unchangeable regularity."

Solomon describes how things happen in life. He seems frustrated because he sees these cycles occur and there is nothing he can do about it. He points out that man works and plans and accumulates and five minutes after his death it amounts to nothing. Two employees were talking around the coffee pot on a Monday morning and one said.

"Did you see where old J. R. Skinflint died over the weekend? He sure was rich."

"Wonder how much money he left behind." The other man replied, "All of it."

Cycles occur and reoccur and they are out of our control. For Cub fans the cycle will return them to a World Series one day. Then they hope it won't take another hundred years for that cycle to come around again.

Big Inning Baseball Quote #95:

So much for the World Series curse:

"I got you Babe!"

**-sign behind home plate at Fenway Park
during the World Champions celebration**

Diamond Lesson #96

Hall of Fame

The act of faith is what distinguished our ancestors, set them above the crowd.
Hebrews 11:2 (The Message)

Can you name the first five players voted into the Baseball's Hall of Fame in 1936? No? What kind of a baseball fan are you anyway? Charter members were: Babe Ruth, Ty Cobb, Christy Mathewson, Honus Wagner, and Walter Johnson. To receive this prestigious honor a player must receive votes on at least 75% of the ballots.

Ballots are received by active and honorary members of the Baseball Writer's Association of America who have been active as baseball writers and members for 10 years prior to the election they are currently voting on.

A player has to be retired at least five years and active at some time during the 20 years prior to the election to be on the ballot. Veterans have a separate election and must have been players at least 21 years prior to making the ballot.

What constitutes achievements worthy of Hall induction? Hall of Fame election Rule #5 simply states: "Voting shall be based upon the player's record, playing ability, integrity, sportsmanship, character and contributions to the team(s) on which the player played." It leaves a lot of room for debating a players qualifications providing endless fodder for baseball conversation among lovers of the game. Just one among many reasons that baseball is such a great game.

At the dedication of the Hall of Fame Museum, Cooperstown, NY, in 1939 Commissioner Kennesaw Mountain Landis' introduction in the program said it pretty well: "From a back lots game for boys (baseball) has grown into one of the greatest team sports in the world. It has marched side-by-side with the development of a great nation. Throughout the world today baseball is the personification of Americanism…American sportsmanship, team play, aggressiveness." That's why Hall of Fame induction is such an honor. You can read Landis' entire text and even hear that first ceremony on-line at www.baseballhalloffame.org.

Watching or playing baseball is an act of faith that your time will be well spent. There are a lot of things that must be taken on faith in our lives. Faith keeps us going, especially faith in a Heavenly Father and Creator who loves and watches over us.

Ruth, Cobb, Wagner, Mathewson, and Johnson were forerunners in establishing the popularity of baseball, so they became members of the Hall of Fame. Likewise there are forerunners of faith in the Bible who are members of the Faith Hall of Fame.

Hebrews 11:1 defines faith: "Now faith is being sure of what we hope for and certain of what we do not see." This certainty has its roots in our faith in God. Hall of Faith members combined strength in the face of adversity with rock-solid faith in God.

Joel Osteen, pastor of the 42,000 member Lakewood Church in Houston says, in his best-selling book *Your Best Life Now,* there are two kinds of faith: a) *Delivering* faith which God rewards immediately; and b) *Sustaining* faith which is an on-going, strong faith that gets you through the tough times. The latter will put you in the Hall of Faith. You'll be in good company as your plaque is placed with those of Abraham, Isaac, Joseph, Moses, David, Gideon, Samuel, Samson and many others listed in Hebrews 11.

To get on the Hall of Faith ballot you must rely on God's promises, provisions, and His concern for you. Faith proves itself in our lives by obedience to the Lord. (QSB pg. 1671). Then, we are ready for the Faith Hall of Fame.

Big Inning Baseball Quote #96:

Kids say the darnedest things even to Hall of Famers:

"It was fun until a kid came up to me and said, My Dad says you're getting old, you're going to die and your autograph will be valuable.' "

---Warren Spahn---
Hall of Fame Pitcher at an autograph show

Diamond Lesson #97

Closer

Looking unto Jesus, the author and finisher of our faith.   Hebrews 12:2a

According to the official rules of baseball a pitcher who finishes a game that is won by his team, but doesn't get credit for a victory, may earn a "save" if:

a. He enters with a lead of no more than 3 runs and pitches at least an inning.

b. Enters with the tying run either at bat, on base or on deck.

c. Pitches effectively for at least three innings.

Actually the "save" did not become an official stat until 1969 and the "blown save" wasn't recognized statistically until 1998.

The pitcher who usually gets or blows a save is the closer. He's the guy who comes trotting in or riding in the golf cart with some intimidating, often heavy metal music, blaring in the background. He's the man with nerves of steel who comes in facing intense pressure which he must withstand to save the victory.

Huston Street, who was college baseball's top closer at Texas in 2004 says: "There is nothing like the electricity of the ninth inning in a one-run game. The emotion and the elevated heartbeats of all those present turn just another inning into a 'pressure situation.' "

In 1990, closer Bobby Thigpen saved 57 games for the Chicago Whitesox. That record stood for 18 years until Francisco Rodriquez saved 62 games in 2008 for the Los Angeles Angels. The National League Record is 55, held jointly by John Smoltz (Braves) and Eric Gagne (Dodgers). Possessing what is called a "Vulcan changeup"—a pitch that dives as the batter is swinging—Gagne also had a 98 mph fastball. Using those two pitches he rang up 152 saves between 2002-04. When it comes to all time saves it will be hard to match the career of Mariano Rivera, who saved 652 games for the New York Yankees over 19 seasons.

Huston Street, who closes out victories for the Los Angeles Angels, his fourth stop in the Big Leagues, offered a good description of a closer on ESPN.com. "His memory is limited to the present, and his focus has a similar aim. When everyone else is thinking about the possible outcomes, he's focused on the mitt. Both success and failure motivate. Ultimately, a closer is a symbol of trust."

Jesus is our closer. He is the "author and finisher" of our faith. When a manager puts the ball in the hands of the closer, he is putting his trust in him to save the day. When we put our game in the hands of Jesus he will save us. We don't have to worry about his failing to do the job.

Hebrews 12 talks about running, with endurance, the race that God has set before us. The race we are running is not a dash but a marathon. There are many snares and entanglements that can trip us up. When our faith is put in the One who will never fail us the game will end in victory.

It's all about trust. The New Living Translation says, "To believe is more than intellectual agreement that Jesus is God. It means to put our trust and confidence in Him that He alone can save us. It is to put Christ in charge of our present plans and eternal destiny." Then the Ultimate Closer will record the save.

Big Inning Baseball Quote #97:

Here's a guy who's not interested in closing anything out:

"First thing I do when I wake up in the morning is breathe on a mirror and hope it fogs."

---Early Wynn---
pitcher

Diamond Lesson #98

The One Great Scorer

Many are the plans in a man's heart, but it is the Lord's purpose that prevails.
                                                                      Proverbs 19:21

Henry Chadwick was born in England, raised on cricket, but came to the United States and got involved in baseball. In 1867 he became the official scorer for the National Baseball Club of Washington, D. C. on their tour. He is credited with creating the first box score and devising statistics to gauge batting averages and earned run average.

Alan Schwartz, starts off his book, *The Numbers Game: Baseball's Lifelong Fascination with Statistics* this way: "When you get right down to it no corner of American culture is more precisely counted, more passionately quantified, than the performance of baseball players. These numbers tell the stories of players and pennant races in a manner that words, photographs, and videotape never do. Baseball and it's statistics are inseparable, as lovingly intertwined as the swirls of a candy cane."

Grantland Rice who would become the "Dean of American Sportswriters" was born only 15 years after the Civil War ended. Rice was writing about baseball until he passed away in the 1950's. He had a different take on statistical achievements when he wrote one of his most famous passages:

> *For when the One Great Scorer comes to*
> *write against your name, He marks not*
> *if you won or lost, but how you played the*
> *game.*

Obviously scorekeeping is important in baseball. Otherwise how would you know which team won or lost and who to give those big paychecks to? Somehow Grantland Rice was able to look beyond the final score of a game and see a larger picture that escaped others.

All of those wins, losses, hits and strikeouts count in a game but God's scorekeeping is a little different. He looks at the larger picture. Of course, He has an advantage because he already knows the final score. That's why He looks for how we play the game, i.e. how we live our life.

Proverbs 19:21 says that we can make all kinds of plans, but these have to fit God's purposes or they will fail. That is not to say that we shouldn't make plans. We should, but they should be submitted to God for approval. Retired Pastor Bob Tindale, formerly of Killearn United Methodist Church, Tallahassee, FL, has a term he likes to use when there are decisions to be made as a church family or even as individuals. He says we should "bathe that situation in prayer." We need to completely immerse it in quality time spent in God's presence earnestly seeking His guidance.

That's how God wants us to play the game. As he says in Jeremiah 29:13: "If you look for me in earnest, you will find me when you seek me." Then the One Great Scorer will write against your name that you played the game well.

Big Inning Baseball Quote #98:

Playing the game right is good, but winning makes the scorekeeping easier to take for this manager:

"On my tombstone just write: 'The sorest loser who ever lived.' "

--Earl Weaver---
Baltimore Orioles Manager

Diamond Lesson #99

Game Over

"Don't be alarmed," he said. "You are looking for Jesus the Nazarene, who was crucified. He has risen! He is not here."   *Mark 16:6*

One of the complaints baseball fans get when they try to talk about the game with someone who is not a devotee of the game is the games are too long. "They're boring," say the non-fans. These are the uninformed, who don't understand the strategies and gamesmanship taking place in the dugouts where managers and coaches are trying to think three or four innings ahead. These are the ones who don't get into the battle between pitcher and batter and the one-upsmanship that occurs in those confrontations.

It is true that sometimes the game can seem to go on forever. How could those fans attending the Brewers-Whitesox game on May 8, 1984 possibly know it would take two days to complete the game? The Whitesox won in 25 innings 7-6 but the game was suspended in the 18th inning, tied at 3-3 and was completed the next day. Final tally on time taken to complete this one game: eight hours and six minutes!

Wonder how many hearty souls stayed to the end of the doubleheader played at Shea Stadium on May 31, 1964? Those home fans who were there until the bitter end were probably unhappy. The Giants won the game 8-6. Oh yeah, and that second game took seven hours and twenty-three minutes to complete.

With length of time it is taking to complete baseball games a person could age during them and maybe even be a year older when it was over like Mark Teixeira did in the 19-inning game against the Redsox at Yankee Stadium on April 10 &11, 2015. The game that started on the 10th lasted until 2:15 a.m. on Teixeira's birthday, so technically he was a year older when the game finished than he was when it started. He was partly at fault. He hit a home run in the 16th inning to extend the game. The Redsox won, 6-5.

In 2014 Major League games averaged three hours and two minutes. MLB instituted new rules to try to speed up the games and in early 2015 they shaved eight minutes off the average time to play a game. A valiant effort is being made by baseball to keep the games from dragging on and to get the game over.

After the phony trial, the whippings, the crown of thorns, the carrying of His own cross, the crucifixion, and burial of Jesus, those who hated Him thought the game was over. It wasn't! On Easter Sunday, Mary Magdalene, Mary the mother of James, and Salome "bought spices so they might anoint Jesus body." (Mark 16:1) Their main concern was who would roll away the extremely heavy stone that closed off the tomb. In faith they proceeded on, certain they would find a way to accomplish their mission.

Imagine their surprise, upon approaching the tomb; part of their dilemma had been resolved. The stone had already been rolled away. Relief was momentary as they peered into the tomb. The body of Jesus was not there. Given the shock of everything that had already happened they immediately thought the worst—someone had stolen the body.

Dismay was transformed in to wonder as "an angel with the appearance of a young man in white…quickly dispelled their fears with the announcement that Jesus had risen. The tomb was empty." (*Believers Bible Commentary.*) "Don't be alarmed, the angel said, you are looking for Jesus the Nazarene, who was crucified. He has risen! He is not here. See the place where they laid Him. Tell his disciples and Peter. He is going ahead of you into Galilee." Despite the worst of intentions, evil had not won. The game

was not over!

Big Inning Baseball Quote #99:

In baseball the game has to end some time, it can't go on endlessly:

"Since baseball time is measured only in outs, all you have to do to succeed utterly; keep

hitting, keep the rally alive, and you have defeated time. You remain forever young."

---Roger Angell---
Writer

Diamond Lesson #100

Perfect Game

Don't be deceived. Every good and perfect gift is from above, coming down from the Father of the Heavenly lights, who does not change like shifting shadows.
James 1:16-17

"Nobody is perfect!" How many times have you heard that true statement? Everybody makes mistakes. It's part of being human. However, there is such a thing in baseball as a perfect game. It occurs when a pitcher doesn't allow a single batter to reach base during the game. The pitcher gets credit for a perfect game, but the fielders are also responsible. To qualify for a perfect game no one can reach base; not on an error, a walk, hit by pitch or a base hit. The first baseman is a lonely man; no base runners to talk to.

As you can imagine the Perfect Game Club is an elite group. Only 23 pitchers have pitched perfect games in Major League Baseball history. Since 1956, when the Yankees' Don Larsen pitched the only perfect game in World Series history, 2-0 over the Dodgers, these gems have been sparse. In 56 years following that perfection there have been 10 in the American League and five in the National League. In fact, if you go all the way back to 1880, there were only five perfect games in the first 76 years of baseball There have been no perfect games thrown since 2012 when there were an amazing three perfect games tossed in the same season..

Perhaps the most frustrating perfect game efforts recorded were by Harvey Haddix in 1959 and Pedro Martinez in 1995. Haddix (Pittsburgh) pitched a perfect game in a scoreless battle until the thirteenth inning when an error enabled Milwaukee to defeat him, 1-0. Martinez' perfect game for Montreal was spoiled in the 10th by a base hit for

San Diego, although he still won the game, 1-0. Both efforts are recorded as no-hitters instead of perfect games. It takes an amazing team effort and good fortune for a perfect game to occur.

If someone could truly give you a perfect gift, one with no flaws that could not be topped or matched by any other, it would be a rarity. One way to determine imperfections is to put them in the light. An object, like a jewel, viewed in the shadows, may have unrevealed flaws.

Our actions performed without the glaring light of publicity may not be revealed in their real state. When they come under closer scrutiny their goodness or badness will be shown. The "only good and perfect gifts" are revealed in the light. James tells us in Chapter 1 that God is the Father of lights. He is the Creator, not just of the sun, moon and stars, but of spiritual light as well.

James says, "every good and perfect gift comes to us from God above, who created all lights." God's gifts don't get covered up or distorted because of shifting shadows or darkness. They are all in plain view out in the light.

Since we are all exposed in God's light, James cautions us to watch our actions. He says to "be quick to listen, slow to speak, and slow to get angry. Your anger can never make things right in God's sight." (James 1: 19-20)

God has given us a perfect gift that is with us always. We read in John 3:16 that "God so loved the world that he gave his only begotten Son, that whosoever believeth in Him should not perish, but have everlasting life."

In the game of life that is the perfect gift!

Big Inning Baseball Quote #100:

Perfection, on earth, was only achieved once and not in a game, but this comes close:

"Ninety feet between the bases is the nearest thing to perfection that man has yet achieved.'

---Red Smith---
Sportswriter, (1905-82)

In the Big Inning is grateful to the following for assisting with baseball quotes & stories:

<u>Internet sites</u>

<u>www.google.com</u>

<u>http://baseball-almanac.com</u>

<u>www.baseballhalloffame.org</u>

<u>www.bbsv.de/quotes.htm</u>

<u>www.sectionb.com</u>

<u>www.lougehrig.com</u>

<u>www.birdsinthebelfry.com</u>

<u>www.boston.com</u>

<u>www.whos-on-first.com</u>

<u>www.sportingnews.com/archives</u>

<u>www.baseballlibrary.com</u>

<u>www.espn.com</u>

<u>http://en.wikipedia.org</u>

<u>www.filmsite.org/fiel.html</u>

<u>http://baseballexaminer.com</u>

<u>http://www.vh1.com/movies</u>

<u>www.washingtonpost.com</u>

<u>www.-word-detective.com</u>

<u>http://www.cwsomaha.com</u>

<u>http://www.niehs.nih.gov/kids/lyrics/ballgame.htm</u>

<u>http://www.csustan.edu/advstd/edtech/4730/Robert/WebLesson.html</u>

http://www.usatoday.com/sports/baseball/2003-07-28-cover-tommy-john

http://www.newyorker.com/printables /online/040517

http://us.imbd.com/title/tt0043967/plotsummary

http//www.americaslibrary.gov

http://www.philadelphiaahtletics.org/history

http://www.quotegarden.com/baseball.html

http://www.historychannel.com (Robinsons)

http://baseballfever.com/archive (Perez)

http://usatoday.com

www.esb.com (Elias Sports Bureau)

Books

Men at Work: The Craft of Baseball by George F.Will, Harper Perennial, 1990.

A Sports Fan's Guide to Christian Athletes, Dave Branon, Moody Press, 2000.

The Mental Game of Baseball: A Guide to Peak Performance, H. A. Dorfman, Karl Kuehl, Diamond Communications,1995.

Speaking of Baseball, edited by David Plaut, Running Press, 1993.

The Yogi Book: I Really Didn't Say Everything I Said, by Yogi Berra, Workman Publishing Co., 1998.

Baseball's 50 Greatest Games by Bert Randolph Sugar, JG Press, 1994.

Sports Shorts, by Glenn Liebmann, McGrawHill/Contemporary Books, 1993.

Cobb, A Biography by Al Stump, Algonquin Books of Chapel Hill, 1994.

1001 Fascinating Baseball Facts, by David Nemec and Pete Palmer, Publications International Ltd., 1994.

God's Little Instruction Book, Honor Books, 1993.

Twelve Ordinary Men, by John MacArthur, W Publishing Group, 2002.

The Sporting Life, published by Henry Holt & Co., inc, 1997.

Babe Ruth, His Life and Times, by Paul Adomites and Saul Wisnia, Publications International, Ltd., 1995.

Moneyball by Michael Lewis, W. W. Norton & Co., 2004.

Big Time Baseball, by Maury Allen, Hart Publishing, 1978.

The Heart of the Order by Thomas Boswell, Penguin Books, 1990.

Ball Four by Jim Bouton, Dell Publishing, 1971.

Three Nights in August by Buzz Bissinger, Houghton-Mifflin, 2005.

Twelve Ordinary Men by John MacArthur, W Publishing Group, 2002.
Rhubarb in the Catbird Seat by Red Barber, Robert Creamer, Bison Books, reprint 1997.

Bunts by George F. Will, Simon & Schuster, 1998.

Magazines

Sports Spectrum, Grand Rapids, Michigan (produced 6-times per year by Sports Spectrum Publishing.

Articles

"What makes a pennant race great?" by Rob Neyer, ESPN.com

"The art of scorekeeping: correctly documenting the statistics of a game remains an exacting and challenging task." by Larry Stone, Baseball Digest, July 2004.

"Baseball to players and umps: Pick up the action!!!" by Mel Antonen, USA Today.

Reference Books

Webster's New World Dictionary, Third College Edition, 1998.

The Synonym Finder, J. I. Rodale, Warner Books, 1978.

The New Dickson's Baseball Dictionary, Harcour Brace, 1999.

Brewer's Dictionary of Phrase and Fable, Blackdog and Leventhal Publishers, July 2005.

Bible Sources

Sports Devotional Bible; Zondervan, 2002.

The Message; NavPress, 2002.

The Life Application Bible, New Living Translation, Tyndale House Publishers, 1996.

The Quest Study Bible, New International Version, Zondervan, 1994.

Believer's Bible Commentary, William MacDonald, Thomas Nelson Publishers, 1995.

The NIV Study Bible, Zondervan. 1985.

About the Author:

Jim Crosby is a lifetime baseball fan and devoted reader of scripture. He broadcast Florida State University baseball games on radio for 23 years, after covering the Seminoles for two years as an evening sports anchor on the local ABC television station.

He has written over 500 devotions, which can be read on his website www.writeman.com and has published three books and one ebook, to date. He has also written one screenplay.

Jim is the District Lay Leader for the Northwest District of the Florida Methodist Conference. He lives in Tallahassee with his wife Susette who has her own interior design firm, www.affinitydesigngroup.com. They are charter members of Good Samaritan United Methodist church.

Other Books by Jim Crosby:

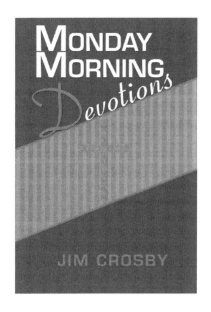

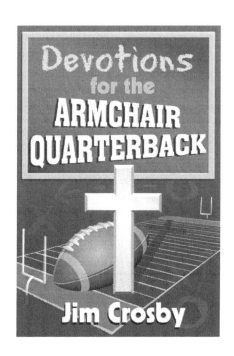

Made in the USA
Middletown, DE
29 November 2015